PATRISTIC MONOGRAPH SERIES, NO. 7

THE DYNAMICS OF SALVATION

A Study in Gregory of Nazianzus

by

Donald F. Winslow

Published by

The Philadelphia Patristic Foundation, Ltd.

1979

FOR ANNE

TABLE OF CONTENTS

i

LIST OF ABBREVIATIONS

ATR	Anglican Theological Review
BHDS	Bulletin of the Harvard University Divinity School
CJ	Classical Journal
DG	A. von Harnack, History of Dogma (1961)
DOP	Dumbarton Oaks Papers
DSpir	Dictionnaire de spiritualité
DV	Dieu vivant
Ekkl	᾿Εκκλησία
GOTR	Greek Orthodox Theological Review
Greg	Gregorianum
HTR	Harvard Theological Review
ITQ	Irish Theological Quarterly
JHS	Journal of Hellenic Studies
JR	Journal of Religion
JRS	Journal of Roman Studies
JTS	Journal of Theological Studies
KD	Kerygma und Dogma
LCC	Library of Christian Classics
LTK	Lexicon für Theologie und Kirche

MBTh	Münsterische Beiträge zur Theologie
MSR	Mélanges de science religieuse
NPNF	A Select Library of Nicene and Post-Nicene Fathers of the Christian Church
OCP	Orientalia Christiana Periodica
PG	Migne, Patrologia, series graeca
QLP	Questions liturgiques et paroissiales
RCF	Revue du clergé français
RevSR	Revue des sciences religieuses
RHE	Revue d'histoire ecclésiastique
RHLR	Revue d'histoire et de littérature religieuses
RHR	Revue de l'histoire des religions
RIT	Revue internationale de théologie
RS	Religious Studies
RSPT	Revue des sciences philosophiques et théologiques
RSR	Recherches de science religieuse
SJT	Scottish Journal of Theology
Sob	Sobornost
SP	Studie Patristica
ThSK	Theologische Studien und Kritiken
VC	Vigiliae Christianae
ZAM	Zeitschrift für Aszese und Mystik

PREFACE

This book is the outgrowth of an earlier study originally submitted to the Faculty of the Divinity School of Harvard University as a doctoral dissertation in the spring of 1966. The revisions since that time have been undertaken in the interests of changing a "thesis" into a "book," that is, of revising the form of presentation so as to eliminate from it those peculiarly academic qualities of unreadability, pedantry, and pseudo-scholarly pretensions. The study has also benefitted from some excellent work done on Gregory since the time of its initial presentation. Of particular note is Heinz Althaus' fine monograph, Die Heilslehre des heiligen Gregor von Nazianz. This present study and that of Althaus cover much of the same ground (conceptually) but are quite different methodologically, and the conclusions as to what, for Gregory, consists of "salvation" also diverge. Yet my purpose throughout has been less to argue with other scholars than it has been to let Gregory speak for himself and, concurrently, to provide an interpretative tool by which he may be understood in our age.

The topic chosen for this study was the result of an attempt to ascertain to what extent the trinitarian and christological debates of the first five centuries were dependent upon or informed by the Fathers' understanding of salvation. It soon became apparent that, with few exceptions, the major arguments and formulations concerning the doctrine of the Trinity and of the Person of Christ rested directly upon a variety of soteriological principles. That no soteriological pronouncements were forthcoming from the myriad of councils held during the patristic age is testimony, not to a lack of interest in the "doctrine" of salvation, but to the fact that "Jesus Christ is Savior" was the one doctrine which served as the irreducible platform for all other doctrines.

But to posit the fact of salvation or to claim

Christ as Savior was not the same thing as explaining the _how_ of salvation. Accordingly, although we find no soteriological controversies _per_ _se_ during this period, there were innumerable attempts to explain how the "salvation wrought by God in Christ" was (1) effected and (2) appropriated. To this extent, the writings of the Fathers are not dissimilar from those of the New Testament in their variety and lack of systematic cohesion.

In pursuit of this further problem, it became increasingly evident that one of the major soteriological themes absent from the New Testament but very prominent in patristic literature is that of theosis (deificatio). It also became apparent that, in spite of the prominence of this theme, surprisingly little study has been made of it. It has, in fact, met with little sympathetic response from historians of Christian thought. Where there has been sympathy, studies have too often been of such a general nature that no theological precision has been possible, or else they have been so uncritically appreciative of the subject that approval has been purchased at the price of accuracy.

The choice of Gregory of Nazianzus as a theologian who might give us some indications as to the soteriological dimensions of the concept of theosis was made for two reasons. First of all, Gregory was primarily a soteriologian; perhaps more than any of the Greek Fathers his writings testify to the fact that triadology and christology have their roots in soteriology. Secondly, relatively little work has been done on Gregory's soteriology, and almost none of his understanding of theosis. Once the choice was made, it proved to be a fortunate one, for in his writings we find, more than in any of his predecessors, a constant use of theosis as a determinative concept for the whole of his thought.

This monograph, then, is an attempt both to provide a study of a long neglected and often misinterpreted aspect of patristic thought, as well as to introduce Gregory's own contribution to our understanding of what it means when Christians, throughout

vi

the centuries, confess Jesus Christ as Savior.

The initial work on this study was undertaken with the wise and patient tutelage of Professor Georges Florovsky. His warmth, his erudition, and his personal concern made a joy out of a work that otherwise could have been tedious. The dissertation was completed, after Florovsky's retirement from Harvard, under the equally supportive guidance of Professor George Williams. During the intervening years when the "thesis" was changed into a "book," many colleagues have provided me with helpful criticisms, provocative challenges, and the nurturing sustenance of friendship. In particular, I would like to thank Richard A. Norris of Union Theological Seminary and Daniel B. Stevick of the Episcopal Divinity School. Too, I shall always be grateful to the late Robert F. Evans for the many hours we spent in exploring the vast arena of patristic soteriology; he has had more effect on the outcome of this work than he could ever have possibly realized.

Donald F. Winslow
Cambridge, Massachusetts

July, 1979

CHAPTER I -- DE VITA SUA

It is commonplace to assert that in order to gain a full appreciation of the doctrinal views of any given theologian it is imperative also to know something of the times in which he lived as well as some of the salient features of his biography. In approaching a study of Gregory of Nazianzus (329/30-389/90) we are fortunate in both respects. In the first place, thanks in most part to the classical histories of Eusebius of Caesarea, Socrates, Sozomen, and Theodoret of Cyrus, more is known of the fourth century than of any of the three preceding centuries of the Christian era.[1] Secondly, with the sole exception of Augustine among patristic authors, it is Gregory of Nazianzus who provides us, within the corpus of his own writings, with the greatest amount of autobiographical data. Throughout his homiletical and epistolary works[2] there are countless observations which give us

---

1. Contemporary sources for a life of Gregory can also be found in Basil of Caesarea, Epistulae; Jerome, De viris illustribus and Ep. 50.1; Rufinus, Praefatio, Orationem Greg. Naz. novem. The earliest Vita is that of Gregory the Priest (7th cy.), found in PG 35. 244-304. For modern biographical studies, consult the bibliography.

2. References to the Orations and Epistles will be by Number and Chapter, followed in parentheses by the Migne Volume and Column. There is no critical edition of the Gregorian corpus. The Migne edition reproduces that of the Benedictine Maurist Fathers, published in Paris, the 1st vol. by C. Clemencet in 1778, the 2nd by A. Caillau in 1840. For studies of the MS tradition, see T. Sinko, De traditione

detailed information concerning not only the
chronology of his life, but also about the
turbulent events of his day. When we realize,
to give a political reference, that Gregory's
adult life spanned the imperial reigns of the
Arian Constantius, the apostate Julian, the
semi-Arian Valens, and the Nicene Theodosius,
the historical value of such observations becomes immediately apparent.

Even more autobiographical material can
be found in Gregory's poetical works.[1] Among
these is the long poem--1949 lines of iambic
trimeter--entitled De vita sua,[2] written
shortly after his retirement from the see of
Constantinople. Here, in the first known Christian autobiography of any length, Gregory fur-
nishes the reader with a kind of poetic vitae
curriculum, including extremely sensitive reflections upon the meaning of his life. These
reflections are so surprisingly profound in
their spiritual and psychological depth that
they have moved one author to assert that in
them we find "an exquisite sensibility, almost in the pathological sense of that word."[3]
Whether pathological or not, many of Gregory's
utterances are certainly deeply personal, and
as such are of exceptional value to the historian who would use them as guidelines in an
attempt to interpret Gregory's theology. Indeed, the failure to take such autobiographi-

---

Orationum Gregorii Nazianzeni (Cracow, 1917)
and D. Meehan, "Editions of St. Gregory of
Nazianzus," ITQ, 18 (1951), pp. 203-19.

1. References to the poems will be made by
Book, Section, Poem, and Line, followed by
the PG Volume and Column.

2. 2.1.11 (PG 37.1029-1166).

3. L. Bouyer, La spiritualité du Nouveau
Testament et des Pères (Paris, 1960), p. 412.

cal statements into account, would, as we shall see, severely limit the value of any delineation of the doctrinal importance of Gregory to the development of Christian thought, for Gregory himself expressed, in these reflective passages of poetic endeavor, the inseparable unity of life and thought.

Given then the wealth of material in Gregory's own writings about his life and the times in which he lived, we must now ask what sort of portrait evolves from our study of these works. The first thing to say is that Gregory saw himself as a man set apart from the ordinary life of the world. A constant refrain, shared by the majority of Greek patristic writers, is that the Christian is surrounded on all sides by the temptations of the secular world. Life is therefore a continual struggle. In Gregory we find what appears at first glance to be an almost "Platonic" disdain for the material and temporal coupled with a fervent desire for a "return" to the spiritual and eternal. This is seen clearly in a passage from the De vita sua where Gregory reflects on his birth and upon how Nonna,[1] his mother, had dedicated him to God:

> So came I then into this life below
> Molded of mire--ah me--of that low
>   synthesis
> That dominates us or scarce yields

---

1. Nonna ranks, at least in the religious influence she had upon her famous son, with Augustine's mother Monica and Chrysostom's mother Anthusa. For a composite description of her taken from Gregory's writings, see Paul Gallay, La vie de Saint Grégoire de Nazianze (Paris, 1943), p. 19f. A serious study of the role these and other women played in the early church is greatly needed.

3

to our control.
But still I take it as a pledge of what
    is best--
My very birth! No right have I to carp.
But at my birth, I straight became an
    alien
In alienation best. For unto God
I'm given as some lamb, some sacrificial
    calf,
Offering noble and adorned with mind.
I'd scarcely want to say: "like a young
    Samuel"
Unless I think of them who vowed me so.[1]

When we say, therefore, that Gregory saw
himself as a man set apart, one must recognize
the twofold thrust of this statement. He was
set apart from the world, but also for God.
His status as an "alien" was based, that is,
less on his conviction that life in this world
is intrinsically evil than on his conviction
that God is good, and that to be with God is
the highest good towards which one can aspire.
The twofold nature of this ascetic motif
is seen in even greater detail when we read
Gregory's description of a vision he had as a
child, a vision in which his having been dedicated to God was amplified and confirmed.
There are several vague references to this
vision,[2] but in one poem the nature of the experience is clearly set forth.[3] In the night,
says Gregory, he was visited by two virgins
dressed in pure white robes. Theirs was a
beauty of purity, he feels constrained to ex-

---

1. 2.1.11.82-92 (PG 37.1035-6); trans. by
Brooks Otis in "The Throne and the Mountain:
An Essay on St. Gregory Nazianzus," CJ, 56
(1961), p. 150.
    2. 2.1.93, 95, 98 (PG 37.1448-51).
    3. 2.1.45.230ff (PG 37.1369ff).

plain, not of the kind that would arouse human
passions! They spoke gently to Gregory, in-
forming him that their names were Chastity and
Temperance, and inviting him to join them in
that realm of celestial beauty where those who
are pure bask in the radiant glory of the Trinity. It was this vision, continues Gregory,
that persuaded him to pursue a life of celibacy and rigorous asceticism. He recognized
only too well that, in this world with its
pressures and temptations, such an ascetic
ideal was well nigh impossible. Yet, here in
this vision, we see the germ of that yearning
for the monastic life that was to color the
whole of Gregory's career.[1]

Still another incident in Gregory's youth
was further instrumental in shaping the dimensions of his future life, an incident which
might be called his "second dedication" to
God.[2] But this time the offering was not made
for him by someone else; he made it himself.
The occasion was a sea-voyage from Alexandria
to Greece when Gregory was on his way to complete his studies at Athens. While crossing
the Parthenian Sea, a raging storm arose,
threatening the boat and the lives of all
those in it. Gregory freely confesses to having been terrified, but not so much by the
waters of the sea as by the danger of meeting
death without first having been cleansed in
the healing waters of baptism. Fearful of this
double death, Gregory cried out to God, pro-

---

1. An interpretation of Gregory's views on
the monastic life is given by J. Plagnieux,
"Saint Grégoire de Nazianze," in Théologie de
la vie monastique: Etudes sur la tradition patristique (Paris, 1961), pp. 115-30.
   2. Or. 18.31 (PG 35.1024f); 2.1.11.162-6
(PG 37.1041).

mising that if the storm subsided and he were
saved he would offer his life completely to
God.[1] He adds that a vision of his danger was
communicated to his mother who, by her prayers, reached out, stilled the waves, and succeeded in bringing the craft safely to shore.

On the verge of manhood, then, the twice-
dedicated Gregory was conscious both of his
"alien status" in the world and of his "dedication" to God. But it becomes increasingly
clear that this dedication to God involved
not only contemplative enjoyment of God; it
also entailed service in and to the world.
Escape from the world as he would like, he
had both vowed and been vowed to serve God in
the "storm"[2] of life. Gregory was constantly
aware of the dangers of such a vocation. He
recognized daily the possibility of failure.
Serving the world meant the risk of being
overcome by the world. For this reason we
can detect a marked ambivalence in Gregory's
public life, an ambivalence which led him
time and again to renounce his vocational
responsibilities and to seek solace and com-
fort in solitude, always hesitant once more
to enter the "secular" arena:

> Nothing seemed to me as desirous as
> to close off my senses and, once
> free of the flesh and the world, with
> my attention directed inward, and
> with no contact with human affairs

---

1. In spite of this experience, Gregory
still delayed his baptism until the comple-
tion of his studies at Athens some ten years
later. See Gallay, op. cit., pp. 65-6.
2. M. Guignet has pointed out the frequency of the "storm" metaphor in Gregory's writings: Saint Grégoire de Nazianze et la rhétorique (Paris, 1911), pp. 144f.

except when necessary, to converse
both with myself and with God.[1]

Yet, at the same time, Gregory was not able to
ignore his responsibilities to the world. Part
of him wanted to be off by himself, engaged in
silent contemplation of God, but another part
of him yearned to share the fruits of this
contemplation with those who were continually
being overcome by the noisome pestilence of
the world. Engagement in public affairs drove
Gregory to contemplative solitude; but the
very nature of this solitude drove him once
more back into public affairs.

This tension within Gregory's life and
psychological character has been described by
Brooks Otis as the tension between the Throne
(of ecclesiastical responsibility) and the
Mountain (of contemplative monachism).[2] And
Gustave Bardy has portrayed Gregory as a man
who was incapable of "determining where he
should be, wishing for solitude when he was
in the world, and longing for the world when
he had solitude."[3] Gregory himself often gave
voice to this conflict. One well-known example
is the depth of feeling with which he described how his father, Gregory the Elder,[4] had

---

1. Or. 2.7 (PG 35.413C).
2. Otis, op. cit., passim. This tension
has also been discussed critically in T. Spid-
like, Grégoire de Nazianze (Rome, 1971), pp.
128ff.
3. G. Bardy, in Review of J. Plagnieux,
Grégoire de Nazianze Théologien (Paris, 1951),
in RHE, 47 (1952), p. 645.
4. Or. 2.6 (PG 35.413AB) and 2.1.11.345-
56 (PG 37.1053-4). Gregory speaks of his father
with affection but, recognizing his occasional
doctrinal errors, praises him more for his piety
than for this theological acumen!

7

ordained him to the priesthood. He felt it to
be an act of "tyranny" on his father's part to
tear him away from the life of calm retirement
for which he had both the inclination and the
means, and so arbitrarily to force this ecclesiastical office upon him. Gregory's response
was to flee to his friend Basil's monastery,
to seek solace in his company, and to lick his
spiritual wounds. But some two months later he
returned to Nazianzus, somewhat shamefacedly,
to confront the congregation he had deserted.
They were, it would seem, not as pleased to
have him back as he had anticipated,[1] which
led him to compose his famous Apology,[2] out-
lining both the reasons for his flight as well
as the motives for his return. Upon reflection
he was able now to refer to his father's tyranny as at least a "noble tyranny," seeking
his father's forgiveness and offering him his.[3]

---

1. Or, so it would seem from the opening remarks of Or. 3 (PG 35.517A). It is unnecessary
to excuse Gregory for what was, in this and later incidents, a manifest dereliction of duty.
Only the fervent hagiographer will assign the
purest of motives to Gregory's vacillation.
See, for instance, Guillon's description in
Bibliothèque choisie des Pères de l'église
grecque et latine, Vol. 6 (Brussels, 1838),
p. 25f, n. 1.
    2. Or. 2 (PG 35.408ff) bears the title:
Eiusdem apologetica, in qua causas exponit,
ob quas, post sibi impositem sacerdotii digni-
tatem, in Pontum fugerit, ac rursum Nazianzum
redierit, et quae sit sacerdotis professio.
The last item in the title forms the major
portion of the work and is the platform upon
which later similar treatises were built, e.g.,
Chrysostom's De sacerdotio and Gregory the
Great's Liber regulae pastoralis.
    3. Or. 1.1 (PG 35.396A).

An almost identical series of incidents occurred when Basil, after he had become Bishop of Caesarea, sought, in a political move against the Arian Emperor Valens' attempt to break up the orthodox dioceses of Cappadocia, to consecrate Gregory as one of his Suffragans. But again Gregory resisted, both the office as well as the "exceptionally abominable and narrow little country village" of Sasima to which Basil had appointed him.[1] Gregory submitted to the consecration, but again he fled, and again he returned, full of explanations, echoing the tone of his earlier <u>Apologia</u>:

> (I was hoping) to be free of practical affairs and to devote myself peacefully to the contemplative life, letting those that wanted such things have them, while I conversed both with myself and with the Spirit . . . I looked upon this present life as a storm and sought out some rock, cliff or cranny under which I could find shelter. Let others, I said, have the honors and the struggle; let others have the battles and the victories. As for myself, it was sufficient that I escape such conflicts and turn my gaze inward.[2]

But, although Gregory gave in to the "tyranny" of Basil, as he had to that of his father, he never did occupy the chorepiscopal see of Sasima, and bitter letters were exchanged between him and Basil on the subject. In one of them he wrote:

---

1. 2.1.11442 (PG 37.1059).
2. Or . 10.1 (35.823AB). On the origins of reflective "turning into oneself" see A. Festugière, <u>Personal Religion Among the Greeks</u> (Berkeley, Calif., 1954), pp. 53ff.

> You (Basil) accuse me of laziness and
> sloth because I have not taken posses-
> sion of your Sasima, nor moved about
> as befits a bishop. . . For me, the
> greatest business is to be free of busi-
> ness. . . and if all men would imitate
> me, then the church too would be free
> of its troubles.[1]

Gregory gave as a reason for his failure to conform to Basil's wishes the need to be in Nazianzus so as to take care of his aging and ailing parents. But even this "excuse" gave him no respite from the tempestuous commotion of imperial and ecclesiastical politics, for, upon the death of his father, Gregory succeeded to the see of Nazianzus. He was not, however, destined to stay there long. If, until this time, Gregory was unable to resolve the tension in his own life between the "throne" and the "mountain," or, in other words, between praxis and theoria, this tension was to be re- lieved, paradoxically, when Gregory was called to the see of Constantinople, the very center of political worldliness and ecclesiastical intrigue. He was called there by a delegation from the then minority Nicene party, and there is no evidence that Gregory thought this to be an act of "tyranny" as he had his ordination and previous consecration. Nor is there any evidence during his stay in Constantinople of that kind of vacillation which had marked so much of his life while in Cappadocia.

It could be argued that once he arrived in Constantinople Gregory was too busy to give any thought to his mountain retreats, for it is manifest that these were extremely active years for him. He began preaching in a small rented house to which he gave the name "Ana-

---

1. Ep. 49 (PG 37.101A).

stasia," symbolising the resurrection of the
orthodox faith in the capital. When he came to
the city, the neo-Arians, under Bishop Demophi-
lus, were in the majority and had secured most
of the city's ecclesiastical property. But,
largely due to the success of Gregory's preaching,[1] the Nicene faith won a following, and,
upon Theodosius' accession in 381 to the imperial throne, Gregory was led in triumph from
his little Anastasia to the cathedral Church
of the Apostles. In the Orations from the period is articulated Gregory's abiding concern
for Nicene orthodoxy. It was this dedication
to the "doctrines of God" which, in spite of
threats to his life and plots to deprive him
of his see, served somewhat to resolve the
tensions in Gregory's life and also established for him the unquestioned prominence in the
annals of church history which he even now
enjoys.

But these few years in Constantinople, as
productive as they were, were short-lived. At
the Council of Constantinople in 381, Gregory's
right to the Episcopal Throne of that city
was challenged on the grounds that he violated
Canon 15 of the Council of Nicaea which prohi-
bited the translation of bishops. The political
grounds of the challenge are unknown,[2] but Gre-

---

1. Gregory's greatest Orations belong to
this period, the most famous of which are his
five "Theological Orations" on the Trinity
(Or . 27-31).

2. Gregory may have fallen out of favor
with some of the Eastern bishops because of
his support of Paulinus for the vacant see
of schism-rent Antioch over the more popular
Flavian. For a further discussion of this
problem, see A. Ritter, Das Konzil von Konstantinopel und sein Symbol (Göttingen, 1965),
pp. 97ff.

gory did not question them. At the height of
his powers he resigned his claim to a "throne"
and retired to the "mountain" of his country es-
tates for the remaining ten years of his life.

It was not wholly without regret that
Gregory resigned his position. Glad as he was
now to be able to devote his life to the joys
of contemplative leisure, his farewell address
delivered before the assembled bishops of the
Council indicates that he left Constantinople
with some misgivings:

> If I have been a helmsman (to my con-
> gregation), I have also been one of the
> most skillful. . . What a battle I had,
> seated at the tiller, as I fought
> against the sea as well as against
> those on the ship, to bring the ship
> safely to port out of this double
> storm. . . Give me rest from my great
> labors. . . Elect another who will be
> pleasing to the people, and give me
> my desert, my rural life, and my God.
> Him alone I have to please, and through
> the simplicity of my life, Him I shall
> please. . . Farewell my Anastasia. . .
> Farewell, O Trinity, the object of my
> contemplation, the adornment of my
> life![1]

But if Gregory was sorry to leave his
flock at Constantinople, no longer to be on
the frontier of the struggle for truth, he
was not sorry to be done with the petty squab-
bling and political chicanery which he felt
was so unfortunate a part of ecclesiastical life. His many satiric and often biting
comments, written afterwards, about "bishops"

---

1. Or. 42.20, 24, 26, 27 (PG 36.481BC,
488B, 489B, 492C).

and "councils" indicate all too well his distaste for that kind of life.[1]

Nevertheless, even in retirement, the "storm" was not over. Although he was to lead a life of relative leisure from this time on, much of it devoted to the writing of poetry, ecclesiastical concerns kept pressing in upon him. It was during these last years of his life that he used his facile pen to attack the dangers of Appollinarianism, much as he had used his voice to ward off the dangers of Arianism while in Constantinople. It was during these years, too, that he acted as guide and counsellor to many in need of help, to which fact his many letters from this period give ample testimony. It is from these final years that we have one of Gregory's most poignant poems, entitled _Epitaphium sui ipsius et compendium ipsius vitae_. In it he reviews with almost pathetic succinctness the tensions that marked the whole of his life:

> Why, Lord Christ, have you bound me
>   in this fleshly net,
> Why set me in the midst of an hostile
>   life?
> Of a godly father was I born, and of
>   no low degree was my mother;
> By virtue of her prayers I first saw
>   the light of day.
> She prayed, and then to God her
>   new-born did dedicate.

---

1. See, for instance, his poem _Ad episcopos_ (2.1.21; _PG_ 37.1227-44) and _Ep._ 130 (_PG_ 37.225A), in which he writes: "For my part, if I am to write the truth, my inclination is to avoid all assemblies of bishops, because I have never seen a council come to a good end or turn out to be solution for evils."

A fervent aspiration for purity
    was in me aroused by a vision
    of the night.
Of all these things Christ was the
    author.
In later life buffetted I was
    by storm-tossed waves;
Against the plots of the greedy
    had I always to be on my guard.
My body was crippled.
With pastors I had to deal,
    pastors who proved no friends to be.
And constantly I encountered
    lack of faith.
When from such miseries I took
    my leave,
How I missed my children!
This is the tale of the life of Gregory;
What is to follow rests in the hands
    of Christ
Who is the author of life.
These words on my gravestone inscribe.[1]

In reviewing the date of Gregory's biography, it might be possible to conclude that
his life could be "summed up as the tragedy
of a sensitive man who entered the arena of
world affairs."[2] Yet we must be careful, given
the evidence available to us, not to judge
Gregory's career too hastily or too superfici-
ally. Tragedy there was, as well as sensitivi-
ty, in his "storm-tossed" career. Often he
recoiled and retreated from his responsibilities. Yet, in saying this, we should not over-
look the fact that, in spite of his many hesi-
tations and vacillations, Gregory did devote

---

1. 2.1.92 (PG 37.1447-8).
2. So G. Misch in A History of Autobiography in Antiquity (Cambridge, Mass., 1951),
Vol. 2, p. 609.

himself zealously and with unflagging vigor to
the care of his "children" and especially to
the preservation and promulgation of the truth
of the Christian faith, activities that could
hardly be described as un- or other-worldly.

Of course Gregory was not alone in his
criticisms of the church of his day, a church
which he saw becoming more and more the captive of "secular" politics. Most of the great
Fathers of the fourth century shared this view.[1]
His personal and individual inclination was to
retreat from the world. This was, as we have
seen, a self-couscious desire, but at the same
time his desire to "return" into the world was
equally self-conscious.[2] In each case the underlying motive behind his return was his concern for the faith. One of his letters to Basil
is a case in point. Admitting his own reluctance when faced with the demands of his own
ordination to the priesthood, he counselled
Basil, who was having similar anxieties, not
to refuse the obligations of a pastoral charge.
Since the church was beset on all sides by
"heretical tongues," Gregory argued, it needed
the trustworthy guidance and witness of people
of Basil's caliber to act as shepherds.[3] Into the
mouth of the same Basil, even after the Sasima
affair had severely strained their relationship, Gregory placed these words, words which
underline the main direction of his own concerns: "For whenever (the doctrine of) God is
endangered or under debate, all other concerns

---

1. See, among other studies, K. M. Setton,
Christian Attitudes Towards the Emperor in the
Fourth Century (New York, 1941).
    2. Misch (op. cit.) argues--wrongly, I be-
lieve--that Gregory did not himself understand
the real reasons for his conflict, believing
them to be exterior rather than interior reasons.
    3. Ep. 8 (PG 37.34D-36A).

must be set aside and our attention directed solely upon it."[1] And Basil, in his turn, recognizing Gregory's passion for Christian truth and his eagerness to set forth pure Christian doctrine, described him epigrammatically as to stoma tou Christou, "the mouth of Christ."[2]

It was this overriding dedication to "pure doctrine" which can be seen, then, as the motive lying behind both aspects, or poles, of Gregory's life. The search for truth led him to the "mountain," while his concern that his flock might be led away from the truth brought him back to the "throne." The "doctrine of God," with all its implications, was for Gregory the one major factor in his life that helped resolve those tensions which might otherwise be described as a pathological vacillation between flesh and spirit, between the temporal and the eternal, between the affairs of the world and the life of contemplative stillness. "Some people," Gregory wrote, with reference to his efforts in behalf of orthodoxy while in Constantinople, "always keep their religion hidden secretly within themselves. . . while others offer the treasure (of their faith) to all, not able to restrain themselves from giving it public expression, since they consider true religion to consist not of that which saves them alone, unless they also share the overabundance of its benefits with others as well. It is with these [latter] that I would place myself."[3] A. Don-

---

1. Or. 43.51 (PG 36.561A).
2. Basil, Ep. 8.1 (PG 32.248A). The Basilian authorship of this famous letter has, however, been called into question; see, among others, R. Melcher, "Der achte Brief des Basilius, ein Werk des Evagrius Ponticus," MBTh, 1 (1923), accepted by Quasten as definitive; Patrology (Westminster, Md., 1960), 3, pp. 176 and 224.
3. Or. 42.14 (PG 36.473C).

16

ders is one of the few historians of Christian thought to have underlined this point; he refers specifically to the "indefatigability with which he [Gregory], whose nature yearned for the contemplative life, devoted himself to the promulgation of divine truth."[1]

But "promulgation of divine truth" could never, for Gregory, be undertaken without spiritual preparation. Theoria was the basis for praxis.[2] A passage from the Apologia makes this amply clear:

> How was I to take on the outward appearance and name of a priest before my hands had been perfected by the works of piety. . . before my lips, mouth, and tongue had been opened to draw in the Spirit, had been opened wide to be filled with the spirit of proclaiming the mysteries and dogmas . . . and had become an instrument of divine melody?[3]

We must conclude therefore that the primary hallmark of Gregory's life and personality was his self-consciously assumed role of revealing to others the truth about the very God to whom he had been dedicated and to whom he had dedicated himself. It is this "theological" factor under which we can subsume the otherwise disparate emphases within Gregory's career. In the De vita sua he describes this

1. A. Donders, Der Hl. Kirchenlehrer Gregor von Nazianz als Homilet (Münster, 1909); see also Spidlik (op. cit.), pp. 128ff and J. Szymusiak, Eléments de la théologie de l'homme selon saint Grégoire de Nazianze (Rome, 1963), p. 81.
2. Or. 20.12 (PG 35.1080B).
3. Or. 2.95 (PG 35.497BC).

element with lapidary simplicity: "My plan is always to proclaim the truth."[1]

But even if Gregory's career was primarily "theological," it was for this reason no less "stormy." As pastor and teacher he was in constant conflict. Against moral aberration on the one hand, and heretical distortions of Christian doctrine on the other, he was continually to fight. Against those whose lives failed adequately to reflect the divine image implanted in them, thereby resulting in an "unmaking" or "corrupting" of that image,[2] against the "New Theology"[3] of those who were ignorant of their own ignorance,[4] as well as against those who played with "artificial theology" as if it were a game,[5] Gregory contended, and with a courage and persistence which we cannot help but admire.

Gregory once described himself, in respect to his theological vocation, as a "talented calligrapher" of Christian truth,[6] and again as a "rational instrument of God, tuned and plucked by the Spirit."[7] Yet he was also the first to admit that his vocation was hampered by virtue of his being a "limited instrument"[8] for the presentation of the great truths of Christian doctrine. Though he saw himself as full of "youthful vigor and boldness" when called upon to expound his theology,[9] at the same time he was aware of how much of the content of the Christian faith is not subject to

---

1. 2.1.11.1246 (PG 37.1114).
2. 1.2.28.95, 343 (PG 37.863, 881), etc.
3. Or. 40.42 (PG 36.420A).
4. Or. 28.28 (PG 35.68B).
5. Or. 21.12 (PG 35.1093C).
6. Or. 40.44 (PG 36.421A).
7. Or. 21.1 (PG 35.844A).
8. Or. 37.2 (PG 36.285A).
9. Or. 39.1 (PG 36.73B).

rational demonstration or patient of human comprehensibility, so that many of his theological arguments would have to be "completed by faith"[1] and much of what he hoped to explain be "honored by silence."[2]

By the same token, although Gregory was constrained to lead his congregation into the ways of righteousness, and although he claimed that no pastor should strive for the purity of others without himself first being pure,[3] he was very conscious of his own shortcomings. He himself had not kept the image pure within him, he confessed;[4] he too was a sinner, totally fallen,[5] and like all others desparately in need of a Savior. This sense of his own unworthiness is well illustrated by Gregory in two of his shorter poems, the one entitled Precatio matutina, the other Precatio vespertina:

> This morn, my God, to Thee I pledge
>   my vow,
> No dark deed will I do, nor thought
>   allow.
> This day I dedicate to Thee alone.
> No stormy passion shall my will
>   dethrone.
> If I prove traitor, shamed were my
>   grey head,
> And shamed Thy table here before me
>   spread.
> Christ is my starting mark; may
>   Christ my footsteps speed.

---

1. Or. 29.21 (PG 36.104A).
2. Or. 29.8 (PG 36.84C).
3. Or. 2, passim (PG 35.408ff), Or. 43.2 (PG 36.496C), etc.
4. Or. 38.13 (PG 36.352C) = Or. 43.2 (PG 36.496C), etc.
5. Or. 22.13 (PG 35.1145B); see also Ep. 171 (PG 37.280C-281A).

True Word of God, I have been false
    to Thee,
For whom this day was hallowed,
    Thine to be.
I gave my promise, true was my intent.
But on this path and that
    astray I went,
Not all-illumined, Savior, by Thy light.
Besmirched, bewildered, kneel I here
    tonight.
Give me Thy light again, Christ,
    make my darkness bright.[1]

The conflicts which marked all of Gregory's
life had their "ethical" dimension, then, as
well as their theological nature. On the one
hand, Gregory saw his vocation as that of winning
people's allegiance to a true understanding
of pure doctrine, and, on the other, he felt
it his task to lead them into an ever-increasing
purity of life. And what he sought for others,
he demanded of himself. "God takes pleasure,"
he said, "in nothing so much as the reformation
and salvation of man; it is for man, therefore,
that my every discourse [is delivered] and for
man that [I celebrate] the sacraments."[2]
This concern for reformation and for sal-
vation--both for himself and for others--is the
major dimension within which Gregory saw his
vocation as one doubly dedicated to God.[3]

---

1. 2.1.24 and 25 (PG 37.1284-5); trans. by
B. P. Blackett, Translations (from the Greek
of St. Gregory Nazianzen, and the Latin of
Aurelius Prudentius Clemens, Hildbert of Le
Mans, and St. Peter Damiani, Cardinal Bishop
of Ostia ((London?), 1937), p. 3.
2. Or. 39.20 (PG 35.560A).
3. It would be a mistake therefore to conclude that Gregory's concern for salvation was
for himself alone, as does, for instance, Hans

Theologically this theme is worked out in
his doctrinal writings; ethically it is addressed
in his moral and ascetical works. But pure doctrine
was never for Gregory an end in itself, nor purity
of life. The telos of both Christian doctrine and
of Christian life is to be found in God's purposes
for humankind, that is, in God's creative and salvific activity on our behalf. It is in the explication of that divine activity (and of the human response to it) that Gregory has made an illuminating
contribution to the history of Christian thought.
The following pages are devoted to an analysis and
interpretation of that contribution.

---

von Campenhausen: "It is as though in his indivi-
dualistic weakness and the disunity of his existence this least robust of the Church Fathers felt
an irresistible need to secure his salvation beyond all 'vain' human possibilities of religion."
The Fathers of the Greek Church, trans. by Stanley
Gordon (New York, 1959), p. 106 (italics mine).

CHAPTER II -- THE THEOLOGIAN

When, at the conclusion of his studies at Athens, Gregory returned home to Cappadocia, he found that his reputation as an accomplished rhetorician had preceded him. He was expected, therefore, to "perform" for his friends, to demonstrate his newly acquired oratorical prowess. But, although he reluctantly obliged his eager audience (and, on one occasion at least, indulged in worldly theatrics[1]), he refused to entertain his friends with fancy rhetorical tricks. He sought, rather, to present his views of the "philosophical life," a life which he described as that in which everything is given up--even rhetorical skills--for the sake of God.[2] Already by the time of the Apologists in the second and third centuries, Christianity, as a way of life and thought, had come to be referred to as the "true philosophy." By Gregory's time, philosophia had acquired several specific connotations: contemplative, ethical, and doctrinal.[3] For Gregory, however, it was the contemplative dimension which he undertook to explain to his audience when describing the "philosophical life." It was for this reason, then, that a reputation for eloquence had no appeal to him, any more than did the prestige of ecclesiastical office.

---

1. Or. 43.25 (PG 36.529C).
2. 2.1.11.265-273 (PG 37.1048).
3. See A. Festugière's excellent study L'idéal religieux des Grecs et l'evangile (Paris, 1932), and G. Bardy, "'Philosophie' et 'Philosophe' dans le vocabulaire des premiers siècles," RAM 25 (1949), pp. 97-108.

It is no surprise therefore that, when Gregory was forced to quit his mountain retreat and turn his attention to ecclesiastical oratory, he refused to let his natural talent for eloquence dictate the nature of his sermons. But eloquence was not to be abandoned; rather, it was to be placed in the service of God and become the servant of truth.[1] As Donders has pointed out, Gregory's great "reverence for the vocational task of the preacher prevented him from over-estimating the value of classical rhetoric."[2] If he once or twice gave in to rhetorical excess, he was as a general rule more anxious to be the transmitter of simple wisdom than the manipulator of florid phrases. "A heavy rain," he declared, "is often less useful than a gentle shower" to the same extent that a torrent of eloquent "words"

---

1. Witness, for instance, Gregory's bitter criticism of Julian's edict forbidding Christians to teach the Classics: Or 4.30, 99 (PG 35.566C-557A, 633BC).
2. Donder's Der Hl. Kirchenlehrer Gregor von Nazianz als Homilet (Münster, 1909), p. 148. Also of value is Rosemary Ruether's monograph, Gregory of Nazianzus: Rhetor and Philosopher (Oxford, 1969), esp. Chs. 2 & 4. That Gregory was successful in subordinating eloquence to his theological vocation has not always been recognized. William Wilson, for instance, had these rather eloquent words to say: " Gregory's productions would have had incalculably more value for posterity if they had smelt less of the oil and the schools of heathen learning, and had more evangelical simplicity, unction and spiritual coloring." "The Genial Theologian: Gregory Nazianzen," in The Popular Preachers of the Ancient Church (London, n.d.), p. 233. Such criticisms often gain favor, unfortunately, by their frequency.

is seldom as useful as gentle "wisdom."[1] The
first wisdom, he adds, is to avoid that kind
of language which consists of spurious and
superfluous embellishments; it is this same
simple wisdom by which the untutored fisherfolk
of apostolic times won a whole world for their
Lord.[2] Accordingly, Gregory rebuked those who
wanted to "feast their ears" upon the eloquence
of his homiletical utterances, since he claimed
to have sacrificed his logoi to the one true
and highest Logos.[3]

That Gregory's success as a preacher was
due in part to his rhetorical skill we cannot
question; but the orations which survive today give ample indication that his reputation
was based no less on the extent to which he
used rhetoric as an instrument of communicating
divine wisdom. When Gregory made the transition
(albeit reluctantly) from his solitary retreat
to his active role as preacher and pastor, it
was a transition which brought the private
world of philosophia over into the public
realm of theologia, where the hidden candle
of eloquence could be removed from under the
bushel and placed high on a hill so as to illumine the surrounding countryside.[4] For it

----

1. Or. 16.1 (PG 35.936A); see also Or. 2.
103 (PG 35.504A).
2. Ibid.
3. Or. 7.1 (PG 35.956B); cf. Or. 6.5 (PG
35.728A-C). On this subject, see P. T. Camelot, "Amour des lettres et désir de Dieu chez
saint Grégoire de Nazianze: Les Logoi au service du Logos," MSR, 23 (1966), Supplement
(Coppin Festschrift), pp. 23 - 30 , and J.
Szymusiak, "Note sur l'amour des lettres au
service de la foi chrétienne chez Grégoire
de Nazianze," Oikumene, Univ. of Catania
(1964), pp. 507-13.
4. See Or. 12.6 (PG 35.849C).

is precisely the task of theology, said Gregory, to illumine.[1]

If Gregory was at first loath to embark upon a career of public theological pursuits, it was due not only to his natural inclination towards monachism, but due also to his convictions as to the nature of theology itself. To be a theologian, as we have already seen, demands moral perfection. "Would you be a theologian?" asks Gregory; "then keep the commandments!"[2] But more than this, a valid theological vocation also demands an awareness of the limits of, and risks inherent in, the call to be a theologian. Recognizing that a little knowledge is a dangerous thing, Gregory has harsh words for those who turned the subject matter of theology into the object of "pleasant chatter," placing it thereby on the same level as the horse races, the stage, or the concert auditorium.[3] Harsh words, too, for those who investigated all kinds of doctrines with the misguided intention of picking only those which struck their fancy, or which they reckoned, with no viable standard of judgment, to be the safest.[4] With equal vigor he showed his disapproval of those who relied for their theological knowledge solely upon "hearsay," with no attempt to undertake themselves a "diligent study" of the scriptures.[5] Again, he took issue with those who turned theological pursuits into occasions for quarrelsome bickering.[6] He was careful to point out, with Paul, that theology is a "solid food," not meant for those who lacked training or whose want of discernment

---

1. See Or. 2.36 (PG 35.44B).
2. Or. 20.12 (PG 35.1080B).
3. Or. 27.3 (PG 36.16A).
4. Or. 2.42 (PG 35.559BC).
5. Ibid., 49 (PG 35.457B).
6. Ibid., 83 (PG 35.489A).

prevented their being able to digest anything
stronger than milk or vegetables.[1]

The limits of the theological vocation,
then, excluded for Gregory those who put theology to unworthy uses. With almost aristocra-
tic insistence he asserted that only those who
are qualified should be allowed into the theological arena: "Not to everyone is it given to
philosophize about God."[2] Yet more than the
misuse to which theology was put, Gregory's
conviction that theology should not be for the
unqualified arose from his parallel assertion
that theology itself is a limited subject, an
enterprise in which only those ideas which are
"within our reach" are proper subjects for examination.[3] Gregory's major complaint against
the "technology" of the Eunomians, for instance,
was that they claimed to comprehend the incomprehensible, and so reduce God to the limits
of human understanding.[4] Gregory, on the other
hand, was often wont to compare the theologian
to Moses who, on the cloud-covered mountain top,
was able only to see the "hind parts" of God,
since neither Moses, nor the prophets, nor any
man could know the ousia or physis of God.[4]

---

1. Ibid., 45 (PG 35.453B).
2. Or. 27.3 (PG 36.16A).
3. Ibid. See also Or. 3.7 (PG 35.524AB)
where Gregory defines "piety" as keeping silent about God since the "tongue" is a dangerous instrument.
4. Against such theological pride Gregory
asserted that God would indeed be "circum-
script" if he were in fact "comprehensible in
thought"; Or. 28.10 (PG 36.40A).
5. Or. 28.17 (PG 36.48C). For a discussion
of this image in Greek mystical thought see
J. Maréchal, "Etudes sur la psychologie des
mystiques," II, Mus. Lessianum, Sect. Philos,
19 (1937), pp. 97-101.

All that is comprehensible are those "manifestations" of the divine which may reach our opaque vision, namely the "splendor and majesty" of God.[1] Which is to say, the limits of theology are to be found within the theologian. A critical awareness of nature, Gregory pointed out, or an astute application of the reasoning faculty, can tell us that God is, but not what he is; all we can conclude with any certainty is what God is not.[2]

Gregory's concept of theology, then, is primarily apophatic. His approach to theological knowledge is through the negative attributes of God, an approach which recognized that the object of such knowledge was always greater than the knower.[3] This can be seen in

---

1. Or. 283. (PG 36.29AB).
2. Ibid., 5, 9 (PG 36.32C, 37A). Even the "heathen," said Gregory, can know something of God through their observation of the visible creation; ibid., 16 (PG 36.48AB). And on more than one occasion Gregory referred to the Platonic view (Rep. VI,508C) that what the sun is to our senses God is to our rational intellectual nature. Or. 21.1 (PG 35.1085A), Or. 28.30 (PG 36.69A), and Or. 45.5 (PG 36. 364B).
3. V. Lossky has defined apophaticism as a "religious attitude towards the incomprehensibility of God which enables us to transcend all concepts, every sphere of philosophical enquiry. It is a tendency towards an ever-greater plenitude, in which knowledge is transformed into ignorance, the theology of concepts into contemplation, dogmas into experience of ineffable mystery." It is not, he adds, a "refusal to know God" but a means of attaining "union with God." The Mystical Theology of the Eastern Church (London, 1957), pp. 34, 43, 238. See also M. Lot-Borodine's

the use he makes of a citation from Plato
(whom he calls "one of the Greek theologians"):
"To conceive God is difficult, but to describe
him is impossible."[1]   Gregory agreed with the
thrust of this statement, and judged it to be
"not unskillful," but suggested that a more
appropriate rendering would be: "To describe
God is impossible, but to conceive him even
more impossible."[2]

The theological vocation, in a word, is
not to be taken lightly; it, like life, is a
"stormy" pursuit. Parallel to the Throne-and-
Mountain conflict within Gregory's personality
was his hesitation, on the one hand, to make
any theological assertions, and the bold assurance, on the other hand, with which he did
in fact make such assertions.[3] This tension
within the theological realm Gregory described
as the tension between the "eagerness" that is
born of hope and the "anxiety" that stems from
human weakness.[4]   It takes daring to be a theo-

---

analysis of "théognosie apophatique" in "La
doctrine de la 'déification' dans l'Eglise
Grecque jusqu'au XIe siècle," RHR 105, No. 1
(Jan.-Feb., 1932), pp. 9-21; and for Gregory's
apophaticism, see J. Plagnieux, Saint Grégoire
de Nazianze Théologien (Paris, 1951), pp.
278ff.

1. Or. 28.4 (PG 36.28C); Timaeus, 28C. A
comparable view is found in Origen (De princ.
4.3.14) although the reference there is not
to Plato but to St. Paul's assertion, in Rom.
11:33, about the unsearchable judgments of God.
I am grateful to Professor Zeph Stewart for
calling to my attention A. D. Nock's informa-
tive article, "The Exegesis of Timaeus 28C,"
VC, 16 (1962), pp. 79-86.

2. Or. 28.4 (PG 26.29C).

3. See Ep. 185 (PG 37.304C).

4. Or. 28.2 (PG 36.28A).

logian, but by the same token it also takes
humility. Yet, more than these, it requires
the gracious assistance of God.[1]

It is for this reason that we can discover
in Gregory's thought two fundamental under-
standings of theologia. The first (and narrow-
er) concept equates theologia with the doctrine
of God, which, for Gregory, meant the doctrine
of the Trinity. In this case, the "theologian"
attempts the impossible by striving to comprehend the incomprehensible, a pursuit that ends
ultimately in humble silence before the divine
mystery. But Gregory's second concept of theologia is much broader. It is here that he
speaks of that divine condescension whereby
the transcendent God, hidden from our cloud-
ed vision, himself speaks to us, reveals himself to us, comes to us. It is here that
theologia is to be understood as the doctrine,
not of God as he is in himself, but of God as
he is for us. This second kind of theologia
has as its object, not the inner life of the
Trinity, but the activity of the triune God
on our behalf. It is precisely at this point
that theologia becomes oikonomia. The "theologian" cannot know God kat' ousian, but God
can be know as Creator and Redeemer.

Because Gregory is known to the subsequent
history of Christian thought by his oft-used
sobriquet, the "Theologian," it is imperative
that we do not too easily categorize him solely within the confines of the first kind of
theologia. For instance, it is often thought
that he is known as the Theologian primarily
because of his five Theological Orations on
the Trinity.[2] But a close examination of these
orations indicates that, while indeed he does

_____

1. Or. 2.72 (PG 35.580AB); Or. 32.19 (PG
36.196B), Or. 45.2 (PG 36.637C), etc.
2. So A. J. Mason (Ed.), The Five Theolo-

speak eloquently of the full deity of each of
the three persons of the Trinity and of the relation within the God head between each of the
persons, the main emphasis of his thought is
upon the saving relation of God to his creation. In a word, Gregory's conceptual theology (first kind) of the Trinity found its basis
in the theology (second kind) of God οἰκονομία.[1] Here, as opposed to the attempt to comprehend the incomprehensible, there are no
rational or logical boundaries to the theologian's task. Rather, there is the joyful offering of one's whole life to God, for, in God's
οἰκονομία, this is precisely what he has done
for us.

---

gical Orations of Gregory of Nazianzus (Cambridge, 1899), pp. xv-xvi, and Ruether, op.
cit., p. 42. A broader base for the title
Theologos (assigned to Gregory by the Orthodox Church since at least the time of the
Fourth Ecumenical Council in 451) has been
argued for; see J. Szymusiak, Eléments de la
théologie de l'homme selon Saint Grégoire de
Nazianze (Rome, 1963), pp. 13ff. Lot-Borodine
(op. cit., p. 35) writes that Gregory's title
of "theologien de l'orthodoxie" stems not just
from his understanding of the doctrine of the
Trinity but also from his insight into the
meaning of the cross; cf. T. Spidlik, Grégoire de Nazianze: Introduction à l'étude de
sa doctrine spirituelle (Rome, 1971), p. 137.
    1. The importance of οἰκονομία to the
patristic theological enterprise has been well
presented by G. L. Prestige, God in Patristic
Thought (London, 1952), pp. 57ff and 98ff.
For a study of the term prior to the patristic era, see the several helpful articles of
John Reumann as well as his The Use of Oikonomia and Related Terms in Greek Sources to
about A. D. 100, Univ. Penn. Diss., 1957.

The truer dimensions of this second, and
prevailing, type of theologia can be seen in
Gregory's assertion that God is seen by us
both through God's "drawing [us] up" and by
God's own "descent," with the intention that
the incomprehensible may to some extent be
comprehended by human nature.[1] Theology, then,
has God as its object and subject. Theology
is a process--initiated by God and responded
to by us--whereby the gulf which separates
us from God may be lessened. God's initiative in this process, however, is not limited
to the revelation of propositional knowledge,
nor is our response to the divine initiative
limited solely to understanding. The purely
doctrinal concepts--i.e., triadological or
christological--to which Gregory gave assent
were all based upon his conviction that the
business of theology is primarily soteriological. This point has been clearly stated by
Leo Stephan: "Die Theologie des Theologen ist
primär und prinzipiell nicht Theologie, sondern Soteriologie, nicht Gottes-, sondern
Heilslehre."[2] Because of this soteriological

---

1. Or. 45.11 (PG 36.637B). J. Plagnieux
calls attention to Kleugten's remark (Theologie der Vorzeit, 2, p. 131) concerning Irenaeus which he feels to be particularly ap-
plicable to Gregory: "La vision de Dieu n'est
pas objet de conquête, mais de pure condescen-
dance de la part de Dieu," as well as to Am-
brose's statement (In Luk., 1.24) that "Dei
natura est non videri, voluntatis videri."
Saint Grégoire de Nazianze Théologien (Paris,
1951, p. 264, n.7).
    2. L. Stephan, Die Soteriologie des Hl.
Gregor von Nazianz (Vienna, 1938), p. 38.
Ruether has also stressed this point in
her recognizing the need to approach patristic
thought soteriologically (op. cit., p. 130).

foundation, theologia does not have as its
principal object either the impartation or
receipt of gnosis; because of this soteriological foundation, theologia is better described as a process by which the activity of
God and the searching human quest become one.
The end result of such a process, as the distinction between the "first" and "second"
kinds of theologia is eliminated, is that God
and those who seek God are ultimately joined
together.[1] This process, for Gregory, demanded
the moral as well as the noetic involvement
of the theologian. It appeared to him to be
a process, however, marked less by a person's
moral and intellectual ascent to divine
heights than by God's descent to the level
of our common humanity. Because the ultimate
goal of all Christian thought and praxis was
divine-human union and because this union can
be achieved only by God, Gregory saw the purpose of the theological enterprise as one of
articulating this union. This "theological"
goal he described in these words: "What the
nature and essence of God is . . . will be
discovered only when that within us which
is godlike . . . shall have joined with
that which is its like."[2] Such a statement
indicates, however, that this union is not
only the goal of life; it suggests also
that there is an original intimacy that
binds God to creation. But because this
original intimacy has been broken, theologia
has the further vocation of explaining how
this separation has been or can be overcome.
Which again suggests that theologia, when

---

1. Lot-Borodine (op. cit., p. 12) has de-
cribed the theological nature of this union
as the unity of the subject with the "objet
de la connaissance--identité d'essence et de
connaissance."

2. Or. 28.17 (PG 36.48C).

33

it operates within the context of οἰκονομία is necessarily soteriological.

It was Gregory's specific genius to delineate the soteriological dimension of theologia, to clarify the nature of our separation from God, and to show how our original intimacy with the Creator has been potentially restored. Gregory's characteristic term for describing that union which is both the origin and the goal of the theological-soteriological process was θέωσιʃ, a term he used perhaps more freely than any of the Greek Fathers.[1] Θέωσιʃ is one of those nodal concepts which almost defies translation. The usual English rendering is "deification" or "divinisation" (Vergottung-Vergöttlichung), words which, as W. R. Inge once said, sound "not only strange, but arrogant and shocking."[2] In this study, therefore, we will retain the term in its original form, hoping that its less "shocking" meaning will become apparent as we proceed. At this point, though it is necessary to indicate that θέωσιʃ was for Gregory a rough equivalent of what he meant by salvation, and therefore was at the very center of the theological enterprise. Gregory himself defined the "theologian"--in his pastoral, priestly and predicatory functions--as θεὸν ἐσόμενον καὶ θεοποιήσαντα .[3] Georges

---

1. It is with good reason, therefore, that Szymusiak (op. cit., pp. 23f) equates the function of theologia with the proclamation of theosis.

2. W. R. Inge, Christian Mysticism (London, 1899), p. 356. The Oxford Dictionary of of the Christian Church (London, 1957) is quite misleading in its direction to the reader, under the entry "Deification" (p. 384), to consult "Apotheosis"!

3. Or. 2.73 (PG 35.481B).

Florovsky has seized upon this concept in his statement that "knowledge of God for Saint Gregory is the way and task of life; it is the way of salvation and of theosis."[1]

Given the clearly soteriological dimension of the theological vocation, as Gregory saw it, it is somewhat perplexing to discover that not a few historians of Christian thought have concluded that Gregory had little or nothing to contribute to the doctrine of salvation.[2] This cannot be due solely to the fact that Gregory wrote no one single treatise devoted exclusively to soteriology, since the large majority of his writings reflect the continuing predominance of soteriological concerns.[3]

---

1. G. Florovsky, The Eastern Fathers of the Fourth Century (Paris, 1931), p. 98.

2. C. Ullmann, for instance, in his Gregor von Nazianz (Darmstadt, 1825), devotes only ten pages to Gregory's soteriology. R. Franks, in his admirable survey of the doctrine of salvation, misleadingly asserts Gregory to have been of "secondary importance"; The Work of Christ (2nd ed., London, 1962; original title: A History of the Doctrine of the Work of Christ). J. Turmel also gives a low estimate of Gregory's soteriological importance, claiming that it "manque d'homogénéité et contient des incohérences qui n'expliquent que par interpolation"; Histoire des Dogmes (Paris, 1931), Vol. 1, p. 356. Cf. J. Rivière, Le dogme de la rédemption, essai d'étude historique (Paris, 1905), p. 175.

3. This is true of the whole eastern patristic tradition; formulas and controversies, it is true, centered around christological and trinitarian doctrines, but only because these sprang from an already existing conviction as to the priority and reality of salvation. As Rivière (op. cit., p. 101) has said, "les

Is it due, perhaps, to the fact that to Western ears much of the imagery of Greek Patristic writing sounds strange and unfamiliar?
Gregory himself remarked once on the "scanti-
ness" of the Italian vocabulary, claiming that
Westerners are unable to understand Greek terms
and concepts.[1] And Steven Runciman, reviewing
the widening gap between East and West that led
to the Schism of 1054, has remarked that "it has
been truly said that East and West could not
come to an understanding because literally they
could not understand each other."[2] But Gregory's
language can hardly be the reason for the modern
assumption that he was unconcerned with or a
non-contributor to the doctrine of salvation.
If neither the lack of a specific treatise on
the subject nor the "foreignness" of Gregory's
vocabulary explains this denigration of his soteriological importance, we must look elsewhere. A review of the literature on the question indicates that the locus classicus for
casting doubt on Gregory's significance as a
soteriologian is an oft-quoted text from his
own writings in which he seems, at first
glance, to deny the theological centrality of
the doctrine of salvation:

Pères se sont souvent contente sur la Rédemption de vues fragmentaires et, pour tout dire,
superficielle; ils n'ont jamais fait de cette
doctrine l'objet special de leurs recherches."
But, he continues in the words of B. Dörholt
(Die Lehre von der Genugthuung Christi, pp.
62-3), by asserting that salvation was less
of a "doctrine" than "le terrain solide sous
leurs pieds." See also G. Aulén, Christus
Victor (London, 1953), pp. 57f and p. 58, n.1.

1. Or. 21.35 (PG 35.1125A).

2. S. Runciman, "The Schism between the
Eastern and Western Churches," ATR, 44 (1962),
p. 341.

Philosophize as you will about the
world or worlds, about matter, the
soul, about good and bad rational
natures, about resurrection, judgment and reward, about the sufferings of Christ. For, in such matters,
to hit the mark is not useless, nor
is it dangerous to miss.[1]

Out of context, it appears that Gregory has
here belittled some of the crucial doctrines
of Christianity, and, to those who view the
"sufferings of Christ" as central to any understanding of salvation, Gregory seems to
have been almost blasphemously casual in making such a statement. "It certainly seems
very strange," writes one commentator, "that
Gregory should consider it almost a matter of
indifference whether a man were right or
wrong on such matters as the last four mentioned."[2] Yet both the immediate context of
this passage, as well as the wider context of
Gregory's soteriological thought, dictates
against too hasty a conclusion in this matter.
If, for instance, we read the very next sentence, it becomes immediately apparent that
Gregory is speaking from an apophatic point of
view: "Our converse with God" is possible "in
this life only to a very small degree." Which
as to say, human definitions on such subjects
as those mentioned by Gregory can never be
final. Moreover, as J. Rivière has reminded

----

1. Or. 27.10 (PG 36. 25A).
2. A. J. Mason (op. cit.), p. 20. See also
E. R. Hardy's similar remarks in Christology
of the Later Fathers (LCC, 3), p. 135, n. 1.
Cf. A. Sabatier, La doctrine de l'expiation
et son évolution historique (Paris, 1903),
p. 44 and A. Harnack, DG, Vol. 3, 163 and
n.1.

us,[1] this passage comes as the conclusion of
an Oration which is directed primarily against
the insatiable disease of the Eunomians,
"wordiness," and is therefore a plea, not to
dismiss soteriological and related subjects as
unimportant, but to treat them with due respect. Gregory's "philosophize as you will"
must be seen, then, against the background
of his major thesis in this Oration, namely,
"let us philosophize within our proper limits."[2]

That Gregory did not intend to belittle
the "doctrine of salvation" can also be seen
from an earlier passage in which he gives us
an almost identical list of topics, but, this
time, since the context is not anti-Eunomian
but pastoral, he indicates that such subjects
as "world or worlds, matter, soul, good or
evil rational natures, the sufferings of
Christ," etc., must be approached with theological caution.[3] In this passage there is no
assertion as to the "usefulness" of being
right or the "harmlessness" of being wrong,
but, seeking to underline the difficulties a
pastor faces in proclaiming the truth, Gregory's concern here is to point out the dangers faced by those who are charged with the
illumination of others, the chief of which
dangers is that they might lead men astray.
Although the "distribution of the word" is
the first of priestly duties, warned Gregory,
it should never be undertaken without a full
awareness of the great spiritual power re-

---

1. Rivière, op. cit., p. 104. On this subject, see Stephan's excellent treatment, op.
cit., pp. 25-30. J. Barbel's comments are also
helpful in Gregor von Nazianz: Die fünf theo-
logischen Reden (Düsseldorf, 1963), loc. cit.
    2. Or. 27.5 (PG 36.17A).
    3. Or. 2.35-6 (PG 35.441C-444C).

quisite to such a task.[1]

A comparison of these two passages, then, when read in their respective contexts, in no way suggests a lessening of the importance of the subjects mentioned; rather, there is here an awareness that (a) superficial theological dilettantism, as in the case of some of the Eunomians, can never detract from the truth,[2] and (b) that precipitous theologizing, when the learning of others is at stake, can lead them to fall into serious error. It would appear further that the first of these passages refers to that kind of "philosophizing" which is done in private, and can therefore harm no one else, while the second passage refers to public preaching and teaching, and can therefore seriously affect the beliefs and conduct of others.

It is also helpful to note, parenthetically, that the list of subjects in each of these passages has to do with the entire scope of the divine oikonomia, of which the pathēmata tou Christou are but one part. Here we have the first hint, to be developed later at greater length, that Gregory did not limit his understanding (as do many soteriologians) of salvation to the data of the Christ-event, but included in it the whole range of divine activity, from creation to the eschaton.

In turning to yet a third passage we find further support for the conclusions reached concerning the first two. This is a passage in which Gregory again lists a series of items which he felt belonged to the recitation of the Christian faith. Included in this list are the Law and the Prophets, the teaching of the two Testaments, the suffering of Christ, the new creation, to mention but a

---

1. Or. 2.36 (PG 35.444B).
2. So Stephan, op. cit., p. 30f.

39

few.[1] The context in this case is not one in
which the wordy dilettantism of the Eunomians
is being inveighed against, nor is it one in
which the dangers associated with pastoral responsibility are being pointed out. In this
passage we find Gregory setting forth precisely
what it is the Christian must believe. The
various items in the list make up, as it were,
a catalogue of Christian epignōsis and are
the "common" elements of our Christian heritage. The last items in the list form a typically evangelical rehearsal of this heritage:
"the Gospel, the distribution of the Spirit,
faith, hope, love both for and from God."[2]
Without these, the "suffering of Christ" included, one cannot be a Christian. Indeed,
anything beyond them, no matter how precious,
is ipso facto secondary.

   The three passages examined, then, in no
way support the conclusion that Gregory neglected the soteriological elements of theologia. Rather, each of these passages, when
read in its own context, substantiates our
conviction that the fundamental basis of Gregory's thought was soteriological. It is precisely because he saw the importance of the
"sufferings of Christ" as part of the whole
divine economy that Gregory (1) warned a-
gainst treating such subjects lightly, (2)
underlined the care with which such doctrines
must be promulgated, and (3) indicated that
all of these doctrines, when taken together,
form the sine qua non of the Christian faith.
Rather than even suggesting that the "sufferings of Christ" were incidental to the faith,
Gregory saw the whole doctrine of salvation,
of which the "sufferings" were an integral--
but not sole--part, as the very platform upon

---

1. Or. 32.23 (PG 36.200D-210A).
2. Ibid. (PG 36.201A).

which the Christian faith stood. These three
texts also provide us with introductory evidence for our claim that "theology" and "economy" could not, for Gregory, be separated,
for the items listed in each of the three
passages point to the full dimension of God's
activity on our behalf, from our original
constitution to our teleological perfection,
from the old creation to the new. And the
diverse elements which go to make up this
oikonomia are therefore not of less importance when compared, let us say, to the
doctrine of the Trinity, but form the very
stuff out of which this doctrine grew. These
diverse elements, in brief, fit into an over-
all picture, a picture which in its total dimensions is descriptive of the divine economy
and which, in its "theological" motif, is
therefore soteriological.

   To conclude our argument for the soteriological basis for Gregory's vocation as Theologos we can turn to a final, and even more
persuasive passage. This comes from his famous
Oration on Holy Baptism and spells out in detail the whole scope of God's salvific activity.[1]
Gregory compared himself, in this passage, to
a new Moses; he saw himself as leading his
congregation up onto the mountain and into
the "cloud" of God's incomprehensible nature,
there to write, with the finger of God, a "New
Decalogue." We might expect that this "New Decalogue" would describe, or at least point to,
that "incomprehensible nature" hidden in the
cloud, but, no, Gregory saw fit to describe
this as a "short compendium of salvation." The
elements of this compendium were not "theolog-

----

   1. Or. 40.45 (PG 36.421D-425A). V. Ermoni
has called this passage the finest in the Gregorian corpus on the subject of salvation;
RCF, 9 (1897), p. 512.

ical" (first kind), in that they revealed the
attributes of God, but were "theological" (second kind) precisely because they outlined,
very simply, the "economy of God," those acts
wrought by God for our salvation. For Gregory, these "acts" included creation and pro-
vidence, incarnation, crucifixion, resurrection and ascension, the second coming and the
final judgment. The purpose of all these acts,
Gregory asserted, was to overcome our acute
estrangement from God and to provide the means
by which our original unity with God might be
restored. Only through these events, Gregory
added, can our hope for theōsis be fulfilled.

This well-known passage has an almost credal ring to it, and to the rehearsal of events
within it Gregory assigned dogmatic importance.
The events thus delineated were for him both
the foundation for Christian morality and the
very nucleus of the Christian faith. An acknowledgement of these events was the minimum pre-
requisite for baptism. If, he continued, there
were other things to be learned by the Christian, they were of secondary importance and
could be learned after baptism, by grace, within the Church.[1]

Gregory once referred to himself as a theologian who was constrained to pursue his vocation whether or not it involved risks.[2] Such
a statement on Gregory's part was not sheer
rhetorical bravado for, as we have seen, be-
side the outward risks encountered in the
world, he knew well the inward dangers which
constantly confronted one who sought to proclaim the truth. The warfare between the inward and outward was not restricted to the tension between the "throne" and the "mountain";
it was inherent in the very nature of theology

---

1. Or. 40.45 (PG 35.425A).
2. Ep. 185 (PG 37.304C).

itself.[1] Yet Gregory felt that precisely in the
fulfilling of the demands placed upon him as a
theologian could the way of salvation from
these inward and outward dangers be worked out.
It involved, as has been pointed out, a tension
between bold assertion on the one hand, and humble restraint on the other; between the infinite
attempt on the part of humanity to ascend the
heights of incomprehensible divinity and the
gracious condescension of God to the very center of our stormy life. Gregory saw this tension resolved, however, only in that union of
the creature with his Creator, a union which is
both the origin and the ultimate goal of the
divine economy. Theologia, therefore, for all
its risks, is soteriological, since it encom-
passes the full scope of the salvific activity
of the Triune Godhead. To review the deeper
content of this oikonomia, as Gregory understood it, will be to elucidate his "doctrine
of salvation." And because of the breadth
of this doctrine as we find it in Gregory's
writings, we can do no better, in our attempt
to understand it, than to start "In the beginning . . ."

---

1. For Gregory's description of the two
kinds of warfare, internal and external, see
Or. 2.87-91 (PG 35.492A-493C).

CHAPTER III -- IN THE BEGINNING

The Christian who is separated from God,
and who therefore longs for God, asserts that
"In the beginning, God created . . . ." But
this God who was "in the beginning" is himself
without beginning (anarchos); and he who "created" is himself uncreated (agennētos). In the
attempt to describe the indescribable, we resort
to the temporal and spatial terms of human existence to portray the God who is beyond time and
space.[1] Gregory will speak only apophatically
of God as he is in himself, stating, for instance, that "there is one God who is without
beginning and without cause, who is circum-
scribed neither by anything before him nor by
anything after him, who is surrounded by etern-
ity, who is infinite."[2] But he can speak more
positively of God as Creator, for here we are
in the realm of the first stages of the divine
economy, in that realm where God has gracious-
ly reached out to create the very dimensions
of time and space which are the instruments by
which his creatures describe him as Creator.
It is in the created order that we have our
first glimpse of uncreated divinity.
   "God is light," says Gregory, echoing a
Johannine metaphor popular among the Greek
Fathers,[3] and, although this light in its
essence can neither be "mentally conceived
nor verbally articulated," it is nevertheless
the property of light to shine beyond itself

---

1. See Or. 38.7 (PG 36.317B).
2. 1.1.1.25-7 (PG 37.400).
3. See the illuminating study of Jaroslav
Pelikan, The Light of the World (New York,
1962).

and to illumine.[1] God alone is self-existent,
alone contemplating and comprehending himself,
but as "light" he pours himself out on that
which is external to him.[2] This, for Gregory,
is the symbol of creation, the shedding forth
of God's illuminating self, with God's own
"goodness" as the sole motive.[3] God was not
content, says Gregory, merely to contemplate
himself, for this would not have satisfied his
desire to pour himself out beyond himself,
thereby multiplying the objects of his love.[4]
It was for this reason that God expressed himself in what for Gregory is the divinely gracious act of creation. He interprets this act
of creation in a manner unique among the Greek
Fathers, presenting us with a description of a
"three-stage" process whereby the cosmos came
into being.[5]

God, he says, first created the spiritual
world, then the material, and finally the human, which is a combination of, or rather, a
"formation" out of, the first two. It is difficult to discover the source for Gregory's particular doctrine of creation; parts of his con-

---

1. Or. 40.5 (PG 36.364B).
2. Ibid.
3. Or. 38.9 (PG 36.320C).
4. For Gregory of Nyssa, see esp. De op. hom.
(PG 44.125-256); for Basil, see In Hexam. (PG
29.3-208). Gregory of Nazianzus claims to have
read and profited from this latter, but in no
way does he follow it; Or. 43.67 (PG 36.585A).
6. Or. 38.9-12 (PG 36.320C-324D). At this
point it may be helpful to remind the reader
that Or. 38.7-13, to which we will be referring
often in this chapter, is repeated verbatim
in Or. 45.3-9. Nowhere else, to my knowledge,
does Gregory repeat earlier material, at least
within the corpus of the Orations.

cept are found in several of his predecessors, but the whole of it in none of them. Yet, whether or not we can trace the source of Gregory's description of the creative process, the motive for the particular shape it takes is manifest, a motive, as we shall see, that is inherent in his understanding of the divine economy.

The first stage of creation is that whereby the spiritual cosmos comes into being; it consists principally of the heavenly and angelic powers. Gregory is hesitant to define the nature of this angelic world with precision, content merely to suggest that it is immaterial and incorruptible. After the Psalmist, he describes the angelic hosts as "spirits and fire."[1] He also believes that there are various ranks among the angels, as well as different functions assigned them. Some are close to God and circle his throne in constant praise of the Triune majesty. These Gregory calls the "first natures after God"; they are secondary "lights" illumined by that first light which is God. Other angels function as "ministrants of God's will," and are appointed to communicate the divine illumination to the lower world, both witnessing to, and, to some degree, implementing God's will for his creation. To this extent the angels play a direct role in the divine oikonomia.[2]

This first creation, comprising the angelic hierarchy, Gregory defines as both noetic and

----

1. Ps. 104:4; see Or. 28.31 (PG 36.69D-72C).
2. See 1.1.7 (PG 37.438-446), Or. 28.4 (PG 36.32A), Or. 38.14 (PG 36.328B), Or. 42.9, 27 (PG 36.469A, 492B), and Or. 45.2 (PG 36.625A). For the function of angels in the divine economy, see J. Rousse, "Les anges et leur ministère selon Saint Grégoire de Nazianze," MSR, 22 (1965), pp. 133-52.

as rational.[1] But the primary characteristic
of this invisible and incorporeal cosmos is its
"closeness to God."[2] As secondary lights, the
angels are an "emanation" from the first light,[3]
and by virtue of their close proximity to God
can see and understand him more clearly and
perfectly than we.[4] It is important to note,
however, that, in spite of Gregory's choice of
words, he does not subscribe to an "emanation-
ist" theory of creation. For all its incorporeality and closeness to God, the spiritual
cosmos is still a creation, and therefore not
to be confused with a platonic "world of ideas"
or an Origenistic preexistent cosmos, coeternal
with God. Ex nihilo creation is specifically
asserted by Gregory in several passages.[5]

There are times when Gregory gives expression to his longing both for the angelic nature (incorporeality) and for the angelic status (proximity to God): "Blessed is he who can
escape . . . this fleshly veil and commune with
God . . . and be associated with the purest
light."[6] Or again: " Oh to be free of the
troubles of this life . . . and to be found
among those permanent elements that know no
variation and circle, as lesser lights, around

---

1. As in Or. 2.35 (PG 35.444A), Or. 27.10
(PG 36.25A), Or. 28.31 (PG 36.72A), Or. 45.2
(PG 36.625A), etc.
2. Or. 28.4 (PG 36.32A), etc.
3. Or. 40.5 (PG 36.364B).
4. And some more than others, according to
their taxis; Or. 28.4 (PG 36.32A). But Gregory never states with clarity how perfectly
the angels know God; see 1.2.10.90-2 (PG 37.
687).
5. Or. 40.7, 45 (PG 36.365C, 424A), etc.
6. Or. 21.2 (PG 35.1084C); see also Or.
8.19 (PG 35.812C) as well as 2.1.1.632-635
(PG 37.1041B).

the great light."[1] There are even some statements made by Gregory which sound as though
he equates salvation with the angelic state.
Once he goes so far as to say that human
destiny is fulfilled to the extent that one becomes an angel.[2] However, he admits that such
a statement is somewhat rash. But if we permit
Gregory an occasional exaggerated statement in
this direction, recognizing his constant desire for that kind of contemplative life which
is similar in so many respects to the life he
supposes angels to live, we shall see later
that his longing for the "heavenly life" is
but a part of his wider vision concerning our
destiny, since we, within the divine economy,
were made to be more than an angel.[3] It is well
to keep this in mind, then, when we come across
passages in which Gregory refers to mankind, in
its original created state, as aggelos allos, or
expresses his desire to be close to God so as
to know him as well as do the angels, or defines his role as pastor as that of creating
"inhabitants for the world above," and "hallow-
ing" those whose real home is with the "heavenly host."[4] None of these statements, by itself,
allows us to conclude that Gregory equates
either pre-lapsarian or redeemed humanity with
angels.

    To the second state of creation Gregory
gives less attention, as we might expect, than
to the first. This second cosmos, he says,
comprises the "material and visible" world,

----

1. Or. 18.42 (PG 35.1041B).
2. Ibid., 4 (PG 35.989B).
3. It is interesting to note that Augustine
in one passage, does claim that our redeemed
status is equivalent to that of the angels;
De corr. et gratia, 27.
    4. Or. 2.22, 73 (PG 35.423B, 481B), Or.
28.4 (PG 36.32A), and Or. 38.11 (PG 36.324A).

the sky, the earth, and everything in between.[1]
The material cosmos is by no means to be des-
pised; rather, by virtue of its "harmony, uni-
son, and order," it is "highly praiseworthy."[2]
There is a radical difference between the two
creations, but this difference is not based
primarily upon the second being subsequent to
the first, nor upon some inherent superiority
of the incorporeal over the material. The major difference, Gregory claims, lies in the
fact that the second creation has a nature
which is alien (xenos) to God, whereas the
first cosmos is by nature akin (oikeios) to
God.[3] There is, then, a definite dualism
which sets the first two creations over against
each other, but it is not an absolute dualism,
since each, in its own way, reflects the splendor of the Creator and proclaims God's mighty
work. The first creation, because of its kinship to God, has nous as its operating principle, while the second has aisthēsis as its primary mode of operation. The first two creations
are separate in the temporal order of creation,
and remain separate until the third creation;
they are opposite (enantios) the one to the
other, and neither infringes upon the territo-
ry of the other; in no way are they mixed,
since each keeps rigidly to its own boundaries.

When we turn to the third stage of creation we can see more clearly the relation between the first two. This final creation, says
Gregory, is the supreme expression of God's
overflowing love. As praiseworthy as were each
of the two previous creations, their formation
did not fully exhaust God's creative goodness.
Although the first reflected the divine light,

---

1. Or. 38.10 (PG 36.321AB).
2. Ibid. (PG 36.321B).
3. Ibid.
4. Ibid., 11 (PG 35.321C).

50

and the second God's harmony, creation was not yet complete. A third stage was called for, a stage which would more perfectly exhibit the divine beneficence. It is to this stage that Gregory assigns the creation of the human race.[1]

Man and woman are a composite nature, a blending of the visible and invisible creations, a "synthesis" of flesh and spirit, of body and soul.[2] Yet Gregory makes an important distinction here. Although the final creation is produced out of the previous two, our higher (noetic, spiritual) nature comes to us, not from the invisible creation of the angelic cosmos, but directly from the Creator-Word (technités Logos). Our lower (material, somatic) nature does come fron the preexisting material of the second cosmos. The higher nature that is "breathed" into us constitutes the rational soul (noera psyche) or mind (nous) and it is precisely there that the image of God (eikōn theou) can be found.[3]

V. Lossky has said that the Greek Fathers generally "refrain from confining the image of God to any one part of man,"[4] but Gregory quite clearly identifies it with the nous. Gregory does, however, stand in the Eastern tradition by his assertion that the "image of God" in us is the "image of the Image,"

---

1. Or. 38.11 (PG 36.321C).
2. Ibid. (PG 36.321D-324A). Gregory is rarely consistent in his anthropological terminology, switching freely back and forth between bipartite and tripartite schemata, using psyche and nous interchangeably, as he does sarx and sōma. See Szymusiak, op. cit., pp. 25-35, and Spidlik, op. cit., p. 101.
3. Or. 38.11 (PG 36.321D), etc.
4. Lossky, op. cit., p. 116.

that is, of the eternal Word who bears in himself the express image of the Triune Godhead,
who is the "definition" of the Father, and who
as Creator-Word, imparts this image to us.[1]
Further, with reference to the patristic era,
although Gregory claims our higher nature to
have come directly from God and not to have
been created out of the first spiritual cosmos, he does not subscribe to any doctrine of
the preëxistence of souls, as did his prede-
cessor, Origen, and very likely his successor,
Gregory of Nyssa. In fact, he quite specifically condemns such a view--without mentioning any
names--as the product of "absurd reasoning"
(atopos logismos).[2]

Our kinship to God, then, stems in part
from the divine origin of our psychic nature.
Gregory defines the soul as "blessed and immortal," as that part of a person which "comes
from God and is divine."[3] Yet nowhere does Gregory fall into the error of confusing or identifying the soul with God. G. Tresmontant has
made this clear in his assertion that, for Gregory, "the soul comes from God, it is divine,
it participates in the heavenly nobility; not
that the soul is, as some have imagined, of
the divine substance; it is by grace that it
participates in the heavenly nobility, which

---

1. Or. 30.20 (PG 36.129A); Or. 38.13 (PG
36.325B).

2. Or. 37.15 (PG 36.300C). See J. Gross,
La divinisation du Chrétien d'après les Pères
Grecs (Paris, 1938), p. 247, n.1; I. Dalmais
(et alii), "Divinisation," in DSpir, 3, Col.
1382; and A. Slomkowski, L'état primitif de
l'homme dans la tradition de l'église avant
Saint Augustin (Paris, 1928), p. 84. Much work
yet remains to be done on this subject.

3. Or. 2.17, 28 (PG 35.425B, 437A); also
1.2.14.85 (37.762).

is to say, in immortality."[1] The soul, in fact, is
immortal in its created nature.[2] More than this,
as we shall see, the whole person is created immortal. What, then, of our lower, material nature? At times Gregory seemingly despairs of
the body and speaks as if it were the destiny
of the soul to rid itself of the fetters of
flesh and fly back to its natural home among
the heavenly mansions.[3] The perishable body
was a stumbling block to many of the Greek Fathers, and no less so to Gregory. But his
denigration of the flesh in the present world
must be read against the background of his
understanding of the flesh in the original creation. As created, we were created as a whole;
the direct and indirect joining together of
the first two stages of creation to form a
whole out of both was the apex of God's creative
goodness. Therefore, human dignity, for Gregory, stems not from the soul alone, but from
the body as well, or, more precisely, from our
compound nature. Though in our present fallen
state the flesh forms, as it were, a chain a-
round one's spiritual neck, and though the body
can be spoken of as the "body of our humilia-
tion,"[4] each person was created to be, and to
continue as, a whole. Our future hope is not to
rid ourselves of the body, but to look for the
salvation of "body and soul."[5] Nor, as we have
pointed out, does Gregory assign the attribute
of immortality to the soul alone; it is men and
women in their wholeness that are both "in time"
and "immortal."[6]

---

1. G. Tresmontant, La métaphysique du christianisme et la naissance de la philosophie chrétienne (Paris, 1961), p. 506.
 2. Or. 38.11 (PG 36.321C-324A).
 3. As in Or. 8.14, 19 (PG 35.805A, 812C).
 4. Or. 2.91 (PG 35.493B); Phil. 3:21.
 5. Or. 14.8 (PG 35.868B).
 6. Or. 38.11 (PG 36.321C-324A).

If, then, Gregory speaks at times pessimistically of his "alien" nature, we find that he also speaks eloquently of the dignity which the lower nature possesses by virtue of its having been created by God.[1]   Though it is unruly, it is still dear to him; though it enslaves him, it is still his fellow-servant (syndoulos); though it wars against him, it is his co-heir (synklēronomos).   The body is at one and the same time a "beloved enemy" and a "treacherous friend."[2]   And again, ". . . though I have called the body an enemy . . . yet I cherish it as a friend because of him who united me to it."[3]

We would be doing an injustice to Gregory, however, were we to limit our description of his understanding of human nature to the elements or attributes which he assigns to each respective part.   The importance of Gregory's anthropology lies not so much in his delineation of the "higher" and "lower" natures as in his understanding of the dynamic purpose for which we were called into being by the divine goodness.   This is true, as Lot-Borodine has pointed out,[4] for the whole Greek patristic era: Adam and Eve had an original beatitude which was based on their potential for growth rather than upon their static anthropological definition.   For Gregory, this

---

1. Or. 14.6, 7 (PG 35.865AB).   A study of this particular Oration, with its stress on the need for an attitude of philanthrōpia towards man's bodily needs, will convince the reader that Gregory's supposed disdain for the flesh is not as severe as many might think; see my "Gregory of Nazianzus and Love for the Poor," ATR, 47, No. 4 (Oct., 1967), pp. 348-59.
2. Or. 14.6 (PG 35.886A).
3. Ibid., 8 (PG 35.868B).
4. Lot-Borodine, op. cit., p. 29.

dynamic element is found first of all, not in
our spiritual or material nature, or even in
both, but in the relation between each. That
we have a "synthetic" nature indicates the purposes for which we were created. It is here
that Gregory evolves what might be called an
"economy of the flesh" in conscious opposition
to those views--current in his own day--which
saw our somatic nature either as an embarrassment to us or to the wisdom of God's creativi-
ty. In one passage, for instance, Gregory suggests that the human soul is joined to an "inferior nature" so that the "superior nature"
would be unable to inherit its divine destiny
without a struggle.[1] The body, as it were,
provides an occasion for us to work against
"odds," so that the reward for virtue would
not come to us as an outright gift but as a
"prize" for victory. The body, in a word, as-
sumes a pedagogical role in its relation to the
soul, testing it and forcing it to grasp the
good through its own efforts. At the same time,
says Gregory, the soul has also a specific role
in its relation to the body, i.e., the vocation, within the compound synthesis, to raise
our lower nature, to free it of its potential
for unnatural grossness, to lead it to its proper inheritance, and to conduct it as a fellow-
servant to God. The soul should be to the body
what God is to the soul.[2]

It is this concept of the third stage
of creation, then, which suggests a "synthesis" of two elements, each of which has
a pedagogical role in relation to the other,
namely, to assist the other in its progress
towards its final goal, a goal to be achieved by the whole person, body and soul. In
two other passages Gregory gives us a varia-

---

1. Or. 2.17 (PG 35.425B-428A).
2. Ibid.

tion on this view.[1] In this case, it would appear, the difficulty lies more with the "higher" nature than with the "lower." The soul, in fact, poses a threat to human fulfillment, precisely because it is the "higher" nature. The soul--in the noetic part of which Gregory locates the imago Dei--was created to praise God and to honor creation.[2] But, by virtue of its exalted state--i.e., of its bearing within itself the image of the Creator-Word--the soul could easily be tempted to praise itself, and not God. Proud of its own dignity, it was in danger of turning against God, of despising the very Creator from whom its dignity was derived. It was for this reason, continues Gregory, that God joined the soul to a body. As above, this was so that we might not reach our goal without a struggle. But, more than this, it was because the soul needed to look to God for help in the struggle. In this instance, then, Gregory conceives the role of the body as (1) providing an element of difficulty, so that we might know the true source of our help, and also as (2) providing an element of correction, so that we might not become overly proud of our own noble stature.[3]

Human nature, as a composite or synthesis, if we collate the passages we have examined, was created by God with a specific purpose: so that God might multiply the objects of his love, and so that we might attain the fulfillment of that for which we were created. The purpose of the third stage of creation we might therefore describe as twofold: on the one hand it is related to grace (since both the fact of creation itself as well as any

---

1. Or. 14.7 (PG 35.865B) and Or. 38.11 (PG 36.321C-324A).
2. Or. 39.13 (PG 36.348D).
3. Or. 38.11 (PG 36.324A).

"progress" towards human destiny are impossible without God), and on the other hand to our "natural" ability (since progress towards that destiny would be meaningless were we ourselves not to participate in it). And the goal to which we are called is a goal which applies, not to one part of our human nature, but to the complete whole.

Since the third stage of creation provides humanity with the incentive to pursue its own destiny and also with the capacity to overestimate its ability to fulfill its goal, it is not surprising that the Theologian here introduces the important category of free will. Parallel to his concept of the "economy of the flesh" is his assertion that we were endowed by our Creator with the natural ability to choose between good and evil, between God and ourselves. Like Origen before him, the term Gregory uses for free will is autexousia. This gift was bestowed upon us so that we might embark upon our journey towards our created destiny as the result of our own free choice. Gregory cannot conceive of our being led forward either by blind necessity or by coercion; attainment of the goal would then be meaningless.[1] As Lot-Borodine has pointed out, within the dimensions of the divine economy, only a free and voluntary realization of the creative purpose, on the part of man, is possible.[2] But free will, says Gregory, is not enough. In the same way that the body was joined to the soul for mutually pedagogical reasons, so too God added to the gift of free will the gift of the law. This was so that our free will would have some material (hylē)

---

1. See Tresmontant, op. cit., pp. 625f.
2. Lot-Borodine, op. cit., pp. 25f.

upon which to work. The "law" to which Gregory
here refers is not the post-lapsarian Law of
Moses, but the pre-lapsarian commandments delivered to Adam and Eve in Paradise.[1] This law
was given, not to limit their freedom, but to
provide them with the opportunity to exercise
their freedom, to determine for themselves both
the direction (towards God) and rate (according
to God's economy, not their impatience) of their
progress. Gregory suggests further that the specific reason for God's commanding them not to
eat of the Tree of Knowledge was that, in their
original and as yet only potentially fulfilled
state, they had not at first progressed sufficiently in order to benefit from its fruits.[2]

When Gregory speaks of our destiny, then,
he is asserting at the same time that for Adam
and Eve, and for us, this destiny is still to
be fulfilled. The "three-stage" creation, in
fact, for all its splendor, is just a beginning. Its real value lies in the goal toward
which it was called to progress. The real purpose of creation can therefore be seen only in
its subsequent unfolding. We were created to be
happy, to adore God, to do good works and to
imitate God,[3] but more than this, we were created to grow. This growth, as we have seen, is
also created immortal, it is a growth that is
infinite in its progressive possibilities.[4]

---

1. Or. 38.12 (PG 36.324B).
2. Ibid.
3. Or. 39.7, 13 (PG 36.341C, 348B), Or.
45.28 (PG 36.664B).
4. As Lot-Borodine (op. cit., p. 25) has
said: "La mission d'Adam avait été . . . la
pleine réalisation du plan providentiel de
l'économie divine." A. J. Festugière, on the
other hand, will describe even fallen man in
these words: "L'homme est un être borné dans

What does Gregory mean when he speaks of
human growth, or of one's progress towards a
final destiny? He certainly does not mean an
absolutization of the first primitive created
state, no matter how elevated that state might
be. Rather, he means growth towards God, that
is, a kind of growth which is a dynamic increase
in us of those qualities which we share with
our Creator, of those qualities which render
us more and more "godlike." Human beings
are, after the angelic "lights" which reflect
God who is "uncreated Light," also called
"lights." But, says Gregory, this term is
used not just because of our rational faculty
or because of our ability to proclaim this
light to others; it is primarily used of those
who are more "godlike" and who approach God
more closely than others.[1] Growth, we might
say, consists of increasing illumination, in
drawing ever closer to God, and in an ever more
perfect reflection of the God in whose image
we all are created.[2] In our primitive state,
we were created as "overseers" of the visible world (second stage of creation) and as
"initiates" in the invisible world (first
stage of creation).[3] But in this primitive
state our knowledge of and proximity to God

---

ses conditions naturelles, mais doué d'une
puissance infinie de désir qui le porte in-
lassablement à s'élever plus haut que lui-même."
"Divinisation du chrétien," VS, 59 (supplement;
May, 1939), p. 90 . See also L. G. Patterson's
excellent article, "Was There a Cappadocian
Theology?" which will appear in his as yet un-
published study on Methodius and Greek Christian Platonism.
      1. Or. 45.5 (PG 36.364C).
      2. Or. 1.4 (PG 35.397BO), Or. 4.78 (PG 35.
604B), Or. 28.17 (PG 36.48C), etc.
      3. Or. 38.11 (PG 36.324A).

were far short of that which was yet to be, a
higher knowledge and a closer proximity which,
as we have seen, form not only our human
destiny in general, but also the vocation of
the theologican in particular.[1] By virtue of
the _imago_ whereby we have kinship (_syggenes_)
to God, and because of our created immortality,
Gregory can sum up the meaning of the "third
creation" most effectively by asserting that
the real significance of creation as a whole
resides in its destiny of theōsis.[2] Each person, says Gregory, is a "creature of God and
called to be God."[3] This vocation of theōsis
is peculiar to us; the "first" and "second"
creations serve as the arena in which the pilgrimage is made. The goal of theōsis is what
distinguishes us from the rest of creation[4]
as well as that factor which marks us as the
potential glory of the created cosmos.

Inherent in the created order's potential
for growth, however, was an equal potential
for failure. The gifts bestowed upon the human
race as the means whereby it could fulfill its
destiny were at the same time the very means
of our downfall. The free will, for instance,
which God gave to us so that our progress

---

1. See Gross, op. cit., p. 246; Slomkowski,
op. cit., p. 77; Szymusiak, op. cit., pp. 22ff.
2. See 1.1.8.70-7 (PG 37.452) and Tresmontant, op. cit., pp. 650ff. An excellent survey
of the concept of man's "kinship to God" is
given in E. Des Places, Syngeneia: La parenté
de l'homme avec Dieu d'Homère à la Patristique
(Paris, 1964).
3. Or. 43.38 (PG 36.560A). See also Or. 38.
11 (PG 36.324A), where Gregory says that man
is a "living being placed here and moved elsewhere and, to complete the mystery, deified
(theoumenon) by his inclination to God."
4. 1.2.2.560-1 (PG 37.622).

towards theōsis might be voluntary, was also
the occasion for our voluntary decision to
ignore the purposes of God's providential economy. We are free, says Gregory, to act in
either direction,[1] that is, either towards God
or away from him, either towards good or towards evil. As free will was the occasion for
sin, so too with the gift of the law. God had
given the law as material upon which our free
will was to act, yet, in disobeying the law,
we refused to acknowledge God's intention as
to the rate of our growth.[2] The potential for
growth was then also the potential for sin,
i.e., the failure on our part to respect the
economy of creation in regard both to the direction of our intended growth as well as to
the "time schedule" of that growth. We could,
in a word, go "up" or we could go "down."
We chose the latter and "fell." The risk that
God knew was involved in the act of creation,
says Gregory, was a risk well worth taking,
for creation was never intended to be the final
stage of the divine oikonomia.

For those who would over-generalize by saying that for all Greeks the source of sin or
evil is to be found in matter, it is instructive
to recognize that, for Gregory, mankind's fall
had its origin, not in the realm of the second
(material) creation, nor even in the third (synthetic) creation of human nature, but in the
first cosmos of angelic hierarchies. In attempting to explain how sin entered into a creation
that was the work of God's "goodness," Gregory
is aware of his inability to give any finally
satisfactory solution; but he does face the
difficulties.[3] On occasion he does resort to

---

1. Or. 2.17 (PG 35.428A).
2. Or. 45.28 (PG 36.661BC).
3. Brooks Otis, on the other hand, has
argued that Gregory could really find no

61

popular explanations, saying, for instance,
that the presence of evil in a "good" world
is necessary to preserve the balance of the
harmony of the cosmos.[1] He also makes use of
the argument, used more extensively by Gregory of Nyssa and Augustine, that evil is merely the negation of good, that it has no sub-
stantial or self-existent ousia.[2] But the predominant view which Gregory holds throughout
is one that avoids, on the one hand, assigning
the responsibility for sin or evil in the world
to the Creator, and, on the other hand, the
easier path of asserting that sin is due to
the grossness of the visible and material creation or to our fleshly nature.[3] He is insistent
in his assertion that only God is without sin.[4]
He is tempted to say that the angelic creation
is also without sin, by virtue of its incorporeality, and at times avoids the question alto-
gether. But he is finally forced to admit that
it is precisely in this realm where sin had its
origin. Angelic beings, he says, are immovable
in the direction of evil, or "at least nearly
so"; angelic beings are near to God, and there-

---

answer to the problem of how sin entered into
the world and thus shares with the other Cappadocians an inability to overcome his Origenistic inheritance. "Cappadocian Thought as a Coherent System," DOP, 12, pp. 113ff.

1. Or. 14.31 (PG 35.900A-C).
2. Or. 40.45 (PG 36.421AB).
3. Nor does Gregory ascribe the presence of
evil (or sin) to the order of "temporality."
See L. G. Patterson, "The Conversion of Dia-
stema in the Patristic View of Time," in R. A.
Norris (ed.), Lux in Lumine: Essays to Honor
W. Norman Pittenger (New York, 1966), pp. 93-
111.
4. Or. 16.15 (PG 35.953B) and Or. 40.7 (PG
36.365BC).

fore "almost sinless"; the nature of God is completely immutable while that of angels turns towards evil "only with difficulty."[1]

But the Adamic fall, which had its origin in the first order of creation, did not involve the whole of the angelic hierarchy; it was with the "Evil One" that the chief fault lay, although he did take along with him several "apostate" angels.[2] Satan's fault was twofold. First of all, it was pride (eparsis) that led to his fall. Because of his exalted angelic nature, because, in fact, of his divinity (theotēs), he thought it only fitting that he should be regarded--presumably, by the other angels--as God.[3] Secondly, as the natural outcome of his pride, Satan's fall was caused by envy (phthonos). This is what turned him away from God--even against God--and resulted in his falling from his created status of "light" into the lower realms of darkness.[4] Once fallen, Satan saw that we too were of an elevated nature, and his envy led him to deceive us in the same way that he himself had been deceived. "We were deceived," claims

---

1. Or 28.31 (PG 36.72B); Or. 40.7 (PG 36. 365B); 1.1.7.53-4 (PG 37.443).

2. Or. 38.9 (PG 37.443).

3. Or. 40.10 (PG 36.372A); 1.1.7.56-9 (PG 37.443).

4. J. Turmel has suggested that Gregory's interpretation of the fall of Satan is based primarily upon Isaiah 14:12-14, where pride is the dominant element. "Histoire de l'angélologie dès temps apostoliques à la fin du Ve siècle," RHLR, 3 (1898), pp. 292ff. However, since Gregory also stresses the element of envy, following the Genesis narrative, Rousse's statement (op. cit., p. 146) seems closer to Gregory's intention: "Le péché de Lucifer fut un péché d'orgueil, mais un orgueil qui s'exprimait par l'envie."

Gregory, "because we were the objects of the Evil One's envy."[1] Satan used his deceit first of all against Eve because (Gregory comments) she was of a more "wanton" (!) nature than Adam. Eve in her turn put her feminine wiles to work and inveigled Adam. And the deed was done. From the "fraud" of the Devil stemmed the first human "disobedience."[2]

The substance of Satan's trickery was to offer us something that was not his to give, something that belonged, in fact, to us, but not yet. "Ye shall be as gods," he said.[3] In the face of this offer, Adam and Eve sought to grasp the very thing that was to have been theirs, had they been willing to wait, namely, theōsis. But their impatience overwhelmed them and they yielded to the temptation. They ate of the Tree of Knowledge and thus disobeyed the one law which God had given them as material for their free will to work upon. They had been created with a desire (pothos) for God as well as a desire to be like God, and this desire was to have been fulfilled in his destiny of theōsis. But this very desire became, paradoxically, the occasion for their falling away from God and from the purposes for which God in his benevolence had created them. Satan fell because of his desire to be "equal to God," and, as Gregory explains, proceeded to steal our natural desire for God and distort it to his own selfish ends.[4]

Just as Gregory refused to locate the origin of evil safely outside the angelic cosmos, in like manner is he unwilling to lay the blame

---

1. Or. 45.28 (PG 36.661B) and 1.1.7.55ff (PG 37.443).
2. Or. 22.13 (PG 35.1145BC) and Or. 38.12 (PG 36.324C).
3. Gen. 3:5.
4. Or. 28.15 (PG 36.45C), Or. 38.12 (PG 36. 324C), and 1.1.7.65-6 (PG 37.443-4).

for the fall upon our lower or material nature. In Gregory's interpretation of the Genesis myths, nowhere does he say that the fall
was due to human flesh; nor was it a fall into
the flesh.[1] Rather, the original disobedience
was spiritual and noetic, free and rational,
or, as he says elsewhere, it was the human
psychē that was disobedient while it was the
sarx that cooperated.[2] It was for this reason,
as we shall see later, that Gregory was so
vehemently opposed to Apollinarianism. A further point to notice is that Gregory is not
so concerned about sinning directly against
God as he is of sinning directly against the
law and therefore only indirectly against God.
The sin of eating the forbidden fruit was
against the "law of patience," and was an attempt to grasp what indeed has been promised,
but to grasp it prematurely and improperly.[3]
A. Luneau, in a recent study, has described
this sin of "prematurity" as Adam's unwilling-
ness to recognize the "constructive nature of
time," and his resultant failure "to realize
that a long preparation was necessary and that
solid foods are for adults, not infants."[4]
Or, as another author has pointed out, man
was created immortal, but within time (so
that he could move infinitely towards his
created fulfillment), but he "transgressed
against the law of his gradual development."[5]

Our common predicament, then, stems from
the Adamic fall, with its origin in the angelic
hierarchy. Here, for Gregory, is the beginning

---

1. Plagnieux has emphasized this point; op.
cit., pp. 424ff.
2. Or. 2.23 (PG 35.433A).
3. Ibid., 24 (PG 35.436A).
4. A. Luneau, L'histoire du salut chez les
Pères de l'Eglise (Paris, 1964), p. 155.
5. Plagnieux, op. cit., p. 426.

of the need for salvation, since our destiny
of ultimate theōsis has been thwarted. Both the
direction of our progress (towards God) and the
"time-table" for this progress (i.e., the economy of gradual growth) was drastically altered.
The theōsis of those who had been created in
God's image was compromised, or, as Rousse has
expressed it, the fall had the effect of "sabo-
taging the work of God."[1]

What, we must now ask, is the nature of
our predicament? What were the actual results, for us, of the fall? Although Gregory
has been accused of being "tantalizingly vague"
on this point,[2] actually he is quite specific,
as well as quite reliant upon biblical imagery.
Having disobediently eaten of the Tree of Knowledge, says Gregory, Adam and Eve were banished
from the Tree of Life, from Paradise, and from
God.[3] He exchanged, in a word, his created immortal nature for his present mortality; the
universal power of death entered the cosmos.
The contrast between the originally intended
theōsis and the newly acquired mortality is
expressed by Gregory by a citation from the
Septuagint (Psalm 82:6-7): "Though we are gods,
we will die the death of sin."[4] Sin, for Gregory, becomes death by virtue of its separating
us from God, and this death affects us in the
totality of our constituent parts; no portion
of us escapes, for it is the whole person that
now dies.[5]

But mortality is not only a punishment; it

---

1. Rousse, op. cit., p. 146.
2. N. P. Williams, The Ideas of the Fall and
of Original Sin (London, 1924), p. 287.
3. Or. 38.12 (PG 36.324C).
4. Or. 7.22 (PG 35.784CD).
5. Or. 2.74 (PG 35.481B), Or. 18.42 (PG 35.
1041A), Or. 37.23 (PG 36.308B), Or. 38.12 (PG
36.324C, and Or. 40.7 (PG 36.365C).

is at the same time a blessing and part of the
redemptive scheme. Like Irenaeus before him,
Gregory suggests that, once sin had entered the
world, only death could halt its progress and
prevent it from going too far, at least until
a stronger remedy was applied. Death, in fact,
was an unexpected gain to the extent that it
prevented sin from becoming immortal; death
"cut off sin" (diakoptō).[1] Mortality, as a condition of the fallen state,is a "punishment"
(timōria) for our disobedience, but a punishment that is turned into a "blessing" (philanthrōpia), given that condition.[2] It is important to note, further, that mortality is not
part of the "natural man," that is, of our created condition. Gregory, like most of the
Eastern Fathers, regards the fall as a fall
away from the natural state, not as a fall into
the natural state.[3] Immortality, as we have
seen above, was, before the fall, part of our
natural condition, not a "supernatural" grace
bestowed tentatively upon us and then removed
because of our freely chosen selfish dis-

1. Or. 38.12 (PG 35.324CD).
2. Ibid. M. Aubineau has described this
identical concept as it appears in Irenaeus,
Adv. haer., 3.23.6; "Incorruptibilité et divinisation selon Saint Irénée," RSR 44 (1956),
p. 37.
3. Cf. Lot-Borodine, op. cit., pp. 29ff, who
suggests that the Western idea of a fall into
a natural state has its roots in Augustine. Yet
nowhere does Augustine, who does say that we
were created mortal, equate "fallen humanity" with
"natural humanity." Human nature, he says, was
created "sound and whole" (De nat. et. gratia, 3),
albeit with the potential for immortality or
for sin (De civ. Dei, 14.13, and 22.1), but
the fall itself was an alteration of human
nature (ibid., 14.2).

obedience.[1]

If the first result of the fall was the punishment/blessing of mortality, the second result was equally detrimental to our progress towards our ultimate destiny. Our sin seriously affected the relationship between the component parts of our synthetic nature, between our "higher" and "lower" natures. After the fall there was no longer a mutually pedagogical relationship between the "inferior" and "superior" natures. Whereas there had once been what might be called a "creative struggle" between them, now there was open warfare. Gregory's symbol for this changed relationship is found in his statement that the flesh, as a result of this sin, had become thicker (machyteros), that is, more of a problem for the soul, and now a cause, not for friendship, but for shame.[2] No longer were the body and soul on a joint pilgrimage as "fellow-servants"; now they were outright enemies. Accordingly, as a word of caution, we must interpret Gregory's manifold statements about the "evils of the flesh" as applying to the fallen somatic nature and not to the "economy of the flesh" as it was originally constituted. The flesh before the fall, Gregory explains, shared in the soul's pursuit of "things above," but after the fall became a "fetter" to the soul's progress.[3] Using Pauline metaphors, but in an earlier time-scheme, Gregory suggests that before the fall the original human condition was one of "freedom and wealth," but these primal human

---

1. For a recent study of this subject, as it is found in the OT, see H. Haag's provocative Is Original Sin in Scripture? (New York, 1969).
2. Or. 38.12 (PG 36.324CD). See also Plagnieux, op. cit., p. 426 and Gross, op. cit., p. 247, n. 1.
3. Or. 14.25 (PG 35.781C).

attributes were, after the fall, turned into
their opposites, "slavery and poverty."[1] Which
is to say, each of our component parts has,
through sin, suffered in itself, the soul as
well as the body, and suffered too has the
originally dynamic relation between them. The
"partnership," we might say, became "dissolved."

A third result of the sinful disobedience of
Adam is seen in the extent of the consequences
of the fall; Adam's sin affected not just himself, but, in him, all mankind. It has been argued that Gregory had no doctrine of original
sin and that he tended to regard newborn
children as inherently innocent until they
had actually committed sins.[2] But, although
Gregory does seek to avoid, out of a sense of
pastoral concern, assigning the "guilt" of Adam's
sin to all people indiscriminately, he most certainly does stress the fact that all of us, himself included, participate fully in Adam's sin.[3]
As to the manner of this participation, however,
Gregory is silent; he nowhere speaks of the mode
of transmission, content to assert simply that
mankind as a whole is fallen, that all subsequent sins are the result of that first sin.[4]

The results of the fall, then, were three-
fold: death, interior conflict between somatic
psychic natures and universal infection. If
Gregory is less than precise in his delineation of the ultimate cause of sin's entry into

---

1. Or. 14.25 (PG 35.892AB).
2. So B. Altaner, Patrology (New York, 1961),
pp. 350ff, and N. P. Williams, op. cit., p. 287.
Cf. J. Turmel, Le dogme du péché originel a-
vant Saint Augustin," RHLR, 5 (1900), pp. 522ff.
3. Or. 16.12 (PG 35.949B), Or. 19.14 (PG 35.
1060C), Or. 22.13 (PG 35.1145BC), Or. 33.9 (PG
36.225B), Or. 38.12 (PG 36.324C), etc.
4. Or. 45.12 (PG 36.637D-640A); ek tēs
'amartias to op' arches.

the world, we certainly cannot accuse him of
imprecision in his diagnosis of the resultant
disease. Yet the realism with which he portrays
our fallen condition in no way prevents him
from asserting with bold assurance that all
is not lost. He is convinced that, although the
economy of God's creative love has been thwarted
by our sinful disobedience, this love has not
been, and never will be, removed. It is not the
nature of the unchangeable God to turn his back
upon us, even though we have become separated
from God by the deceit of the Devil and the
sharp taste of sin.[1]

The economy of creation involved, as we have
seen, a risk on the part of God, a risk that God
both foresaw and was willing to take. This risk
was centered in the created and voluntary potential for growth towards good or towards evil. But
no risk, in fact, could be so great as to be able
ultimately to prevent God from doing something
about it. We could not, as the prime object of
God's love, be so "utterly ruined" as to be beyond
the reach of God's help.[2] And the help now needed for our common predicament could come from
no other source than from the very God who was
both the origin and the final goal of our intended progress towards theōsis. The fall of
the created orders called for what Gregory often
refers to as a "new creation" or "re-creation"
(anaplasis), a creation, in fact, "more godlike
and exalted" than the first.[3] The means by which
God chose to effect this new creation was to
send a New Adam to save the Old,[4] to inject into
the created order the "archetype" of the Image
that had been created in us but was now, if
not totally destroyed, at least seriously tar-

---

1. Or. 39.13 (PG 35.348D).
2. Ibid., and Or. 37.13 (PG 36.298B).
3. Or. 40.7 (PG 36.365C).
4. Or. 39.13 (PG 35.349AB).

nished.[1] The economy of re-creation will be,
as Gregory understands it, an economy of salvation in which both the sin of disobedience
as well as the results of that sin will be
dealt with. Sin caused the fall and must some-
how be overcome. But, as Athanasius had often
pointed out, the removal of sin cannot be
enough if the results of that sin remain, if,
that is, we continue in a mortal and perishable condition.[2] Re-creation, in a word,
must be so effected that the results of the
fall, as well as its cause, are addressed.
Death must be conquered, the cooperating relationship between body and soul must be restored, and a cure found, not just for the
individual, but for the whole of humankind,
universally.[3]

The burden of Gregory's concern, in his interpretation of the fall, is less to point out
the seriousness of our predicament than to
proclaim that God, in what we may now refer
to as the "economy of salvation," has himself
acted on our behalf, and that our created
potential for growth towards our ultimate
destiny of theōsis has, in Jesus Christ, been
restored. The manifold dimensions of Gregory's
interpretation of how this has been done will
be the subject of the next four chapters.

---

1. Or. 4.78 (PG 35.604B).
2. This point, frequently asserted by the
Greek Fathers, finds its best known articulation in Athanasius, De Inc. 7.
3. Or. 16.15 (PG 35.953C), Or. 32.22 (PG
36.200B) and Or. 39.13 (PG 36.348D).

71

CHAPTER IV -- THE ECONOMY OF THE BODY OF CHRIST

Part One -- Life

Once Adam--and with him all of mankind--had
fallen from his natural created state, God took
immediate corrective action. On the one hand,
after expelling them from the Garden, he chas-
tised them over the years with a series of calam-
ities. Plagues, floods, and wars were visited
upon them with the primary purpose of inducing
them to turn from their sin. This punishment was
applied therapeutically, says Gregory, as he hap-
pily quotes the familiar Proverb: "Whom the Lord
loves he corrects."[1] On the other hand, God also
sustained them by the means of gifts which were
necessary to them in their fallen condition, gifts
without which they would not have been able to
survive. Among these it was the Law and Prophets
that were the prime instruments of God's providential care.[2] This combination of corrective punishment and compassionate sustenance, of "wrath and
mercy," had as its final goal the destruction
of both the root and the branch of that evil
which had sprung up in creation.[3] This places

---

1. Prov. 3:12 (LXX) in Or. 16.15 (PG 35.
956A); see also Or. 38.13 (PG 36.325A) and Or.
40.9 (PG 36.369AB).
2. Or. 38.13 (PG 36.325A). In one passage
Gregory refers to the two Testaments as two
"earthquakes," i.e., the two most important
events in the history of humanity: (a) the change
from idolatry to Law, and (b) the change from Law
to Gospel; Or. 31.25 (PG 36.149BC). A. Luneau
(op. cit., pp. 151ff) has seen in these symbols
the key to Gregory's concept of Heilsgeschichte.
3. Or. 38.13 (PG 36.325A).

Gregory within the school of interpreters who
see the events related in the Old Testament as
an undeniable part of God's redemptive activity
on behalf of humanity.

But, Gregory has to admit, these initial
steps were not successful; God's methods were,
in fact, a failure, at least at this stage of
the oikonomia. The "disease," instead of get-
ting better, grew worse, and the sinfulness of
mankind became alarmingly aggravated. Idolatry
became the major barrier to "re-creation" and
the symbol of the increasing separation from
God, for it was the transfer of worship from
the Creator (pepoiēkōs) to the creature (ktisma)
that indicated how far from God we had fallen.
Therefore, says Gregory, a stronger remedy
(pharmakon) and a more effective help (boēthēma)
were needed.[1] And these, he continues, were provided. The remedy of which Gregory speaks was
the incarnation (enanthrōpēsis), the descent of
God himself directly into the human situation
and his assumption of human nature.[2] The incarnation was the means whereby the agent of creation became also the agent of re-creation, for
the incarnation has but one motive, salvation.[3]
And because salvation is the restoration to us
of our originally intended potential for growth
towards our ultimate destiny, creation and salvation are intrinsically related in respect to
the providential purposes of God for us.

It is for this reason that the Creator-
Redeemer, for Gregory, is no Philonic demiurge
or emanation; he is neither separate from the
Father nor subordinate to him. The very key
to salvation, Gregory asserts, is that Jesus
Christ, the incarnate Logos tou Theou, is

---

1. Or. 38.13 (PG 36.325A).
2. Ibid. (PG 36.325B).
3. Or. 34.10 (PG 36.252A), etc.

God;[1] to confess Christ as God is, in fact,
precisely what distinguished one as a Christian, and therefore as the inheritor of the
creative-redemptive promises of God.[2]

In his explication of the relation of
Christ to the triune Godhead, Gregory holds
fast to the Nicene assertion that the Son is
homoousios to the Father. And when we remember that, for Gregory as for most of the Eastern Fathers, "God" is the word by which the
triune Godhead is signified--and not, as is
more common in the West, God the Father--the
implications of this credal fidelity are wider
than perhaps even the Fathers at Nicaea ever
imagined.[3] Gregory quite consciously attempts
to steer a middle course between Sabellian
conservatism on the one hand and Arian liberal-
ism on the other.[4] In Sabellianism, he claims,
there is the danger of so closely identifying
the persons of the Trinity (in the interests
of preserving the monarchia of God) that the
necessary distinction between them is obliterated. And in the "mania" of Arianism there is
the danger of so separating the persons of
the Trinity (in the interests of preserving
the unique ingenerate nature of the Father)
that there remains no real relation between

---

1. Or. 33.16-7 (PG 36.223C-236C).
2. Or. 37.17 (PG 36.301C).
3. See, for instance, Or. 38.8 (PG 36.
320B): "Whenever I say God, I mean Father,
Son, and Holy Spirit." On the difficulties
inherent in the Nicene assertion of consubstantiality, see M. F. Wiles, "The Doctrine
of Christ in the Patristic Age," in Pittenger
(ed.), Christ for us Today (London, 1968),
pp. 81-90.
4. Or. 2.36-7 (PG 35.444B-445B), Or. 21.13
(PG 35.1096A-C), Or. 34.8 (PG 36.248D-249A),
Or. 38.8, 15 (PG 36.320A-C), 328C-329B), etc.

them at all. Sabellianism, in a word, is an heretical contraction (sustolē) of the Deity, while Arianism is an unnatural mutilation (katatomē) of it.[1] Sabellianism wants to "fuse" God together; Arianism wants to "cut him into parts."[2]

Gregory's middle course, then, is an attempt at one and the same time to assert the monarchia of the Godhead as well as to maintain the distinction between the persons of the Godhead, a balance that subsequent generations of Christians would identify with "orthodoxy." That such a balance does not lend itself to "logical" formulation does not appear to be of concern to Gregory. A characteristic expression by which he seeks to articulate the middle course between the two major trinitarian heresies is his statement that the Deity is "divided without division" and "united in division."[3] He follows this with the soon to become traditional formula: "For the Deity is one in three, and the three are one."[4] Yet we cannot accuse Gregory of merely playing with words.[5]

---

1. Or. 21.13 (PG 35.1096B).
2. Or. 39.11 (PG 36.348A).
3. Ibid. (PG 36.345CD).
4. Ibid.
5. It is not our purpose in this chapter to give a complete account of Gregory's triadological and christological views; we will confine ourselves, rather, to those major emphases within his thought which are of particular relevance to his soteriology. A helpful discussion of the issues involved here will be found in G. L. Prestige (op. cit.), esp. Chs. 11 & 12; see also A. Grillmeier's monograph, "Die theologische und sprachliche Vorbereitung der christologischen Formel von Chalkedon," in A. Grillmeier and H. Dacht (eds.), Das Konzil von Chalkedon (Würzburg, 1951), pp. 5-202.

His intention is to point out, not that the
Son is the same as the Father (this would be
in the direction of Sabellianism), but that
the Son is as much God as the Father is. The
Father is God; so too is the Son. This becomes
clear when Gregory goes on to suggest that the
words "Father" and "Son" do not in themselves
describe the ousia of an individuated hypostasis; rather, they are used to indicate the relation (schesis) between them, as well as the
specific characteristics (idiotēs) of each.[1]
As to the relation, for instance, the Father
is related to the Son as a Father; as to his
characteristics, he is distinct from the Son
in that he is not the Son, but a Father. Yet
both Father and Son share equally in the same
Deity, their common ousia is that of the Godhead, and therefore each has a "common name,"
i.e., "God."[2]

    J. N. D. Kelly has pointed out that Gre-
gory's significance here lies in his concern
to shift the trinitarian emphasis from a
"numerical" unity (which the Arians were quick
to recognize as illogical) to a unity of "nature."[3] But with the unity of the Godhead
fully established, Gregory is still at pains
further to articulate the distinction between
persons, and, in this case, the specific relation between Father and Son. On the one hand,
he will describe the Father as gennētōr and
the Son as gennēma,[4] or the Father as anarchos and the Son as gennētos.[5] On the other

---

    1. Or. 21.16 (PG 36.96A) and Or. 31.19 (PG
36.153B0156A).
    2. Or. 29.4 (PG 36.77C-80A) and Or. 33.17
(PG 36.236C).
    3. J. N. D. Kelly, Early Christian Doc-
trines (New York, 1958), p. 268.
    4. Or. 29.2 (PG 36.76B).
    5. Or. 39.12 (PG 36.348B).

hand, he will insist (again with the Arians in mind) that this relation is effected "impassibly, beyond the category of time, and with no reference to corporeality" (apathōs, achronōs, and asōmatōs).[1] The Father indeed "generates" or "begets" the Son, but this in no way means that the "cause" is prior to its "effect." Time, mutability, corporeality, causality, and such concepts, claims Gregory, are used of the relation between Father and Son only by those who are "bad umpires and measurers of the Godhead."[2] The generation of the Son, he goes on to say, cannot be construed as to make him subordinate or inferior to the Father; rather, it is a term used merely to distinguish him from the Father.[3] In spite of such rigorous argumentation, it must be admitted that Gregory is aware of his inability to be as precise as he would like to be. This is particularly true when he concludes--we can almost hear a sigh!-- that the "generation of the Son" is a mystery known only "to the Father who begat and to the Son who was begotten."[4]

Gregory's insistence on the full deity of the preëxistent Son or Logos (who is coëternal with the Father and participates equally with the Father in the "substance" of the Godhead) is manifestly soteriological. Since it was God who created the world, so too it must be God who re-creates it. The ultimate hope of the created cosmos can never be placed in a "crea-

-----

1. Or. 29.2 (PG 36.76B).
2. Ibid., 3 (PG 36.77AB) and Or. 3.6 (PG 35.521C).
3. Or. 29.3-5 (PG 36.77A-80B).
4. Or. 29.8 (PG 36.84C). Cf. Irenaeus, Adv. haer., 3.28.6: "Si quis itaque nobis dixerit: Quomodo ergo Filius prolatus a Patre est? dicimus ei, quia prolationem istam . . . inenerrabilem, nemo novit nisi solus qui generavit Pater, et qui natus est Filius."

ture." The author of the divine oikonomia is--
and can be no other than--God. Therefore, the
full deity of the Son, who is Savior, must be
preserved.[1]

But this is not all. Since it is we who
need to be saved, and only God can save, the
Savior must be God. Yet, because it is we who
need to be saved, the Savior must also be one
of us. This assertion, common in Irenaeus and
Athanasius, is taken for granted in Gregory and
therefore seldom spelled out in detail. Karl
Holl has paraphrased Gregory's view here with
the statement that " . . . if the redeemer is
not at one and the same time God and man, then
a valid atonement is either not fully effected,
or not fully effected for man."[2] It is, then,
the same soteriological concern that underlies
Gregory's confession of both the full deity and
the full humanity of the Savior, the incarnate
Son of God. It is this latter that forms the
basis of Gregory's passionate defence of "orthodoxy" against the christological formulas of
Apollinarianism. As early as 362, a full two de-
cades before he undertook publicly to expose
the heresy of Apollinaris and his followers, Gregory writes that, in Christ, God was united to
full man, i.e., to body and soul.[3] In Gregory's

---

1. Or. 35.17 (PG 36.301BC), etc. For the soteriological basis of the Son's deity, see F. M.
Young, "Christological Ideas in the Greek Commentaries on the Epistle to the Hebrews," JTS,
20 (Part 1; 1969), pp. 150-63.
2. Karl Holl, Amphilochius von Ikonium in
seinem Verhältnis zu den grossen Kappadoziern
(Tübingen, 1904), p. 182.
3. Or. 2.23 (PG 35.432C-433A). In Gregory's
correspondence with Cledonius (Ep. 102), he
claims Apollinarianism to have arisen "thirty
years earlier," i.e., ca. 352. Therefore, although he refers in Ep. 101 to Apollinarianism

view, the Apollinarian Christ is no Savior at
all. How can the Logos, if joined to only a
part of man, save the whole man? The incarnation, he repeats, must effect a full union with
man in his fullness; the incarnate Logos must
be "whole man and also be God" for the sake of
the "whole sufferer."[1] When Apollinaris has the
Logos assume the role of, or even replace, the
noetic soul or mind in Christ, leaving only
the flesh and the animal soul truly human, he
is guilty of refusing salvation, says Gregory,
to that very element in the human constitution
which stands in need of the most help, the very
place where, as we have already noticed, sin
entered in.[2] A Savior without a human nous is
no Savior at all. Gregory wants God's assumption of human nature to benefit him in his
wholeness; he wants to see a true enanthrōpēsis. Godhead joined to flesh and animal soul
is not man; unless there also is a nous, there is
no anthrōpos.[3]
    The motive behind Apollinaris' christology,
we must admit, was as much soteriological as
that which informed Gregory's concept of the
person of Christ. But in their respective formulations there was a marked difference. Whereas
Gregory's emphasis was on the completeness of

---

as an "innovation," since this was often a term
of abuse classically applied to heresy, we cannot conclude that this heresy was therefore new
to Gregory. For this and related issues see J.
Dräseke's still helpful monograph, "Gregorios
von Nazianz und sein Verhältnis zum Apollinarismus," ThSK, 65 (1892), pp. 473-512, and E.
Mühlenberg's recent study, Apollinaris von Laodicea (Göttingen, 1969).
    1. Or. 40.45 (PG 36.421B).
    2. Ep. 101 (PG 37.188B).
    3. Ibid. (PG 37.184B) and 1.1.10.1-4 (PG
37.464-5).

the Logos' assumption of human nature, Apollinaris appears to have been chiefly concerned
with the "balanced and logical" result of such
assumption. Apollinaris' rigorous metaphysical
logic led him to deny the completeness of
Christ's human nature because, as Gregory was
only too willing to point out, he was unable
to comprehend how two measures of something
could fit into a one-measure container.[1] Whether Apollinaris' refusal to assign a human
nous to the incarnate Logos was because he felt
it to be beyond salvation, because of its so-
called "filthy imaginations," or because he
thought it stood in no intrinsic need of salvation, by virtue of its noetic and therefore
immaterial nature, is difficult to ascertain.[2]
But the main point is quite clear: the danger
in Apollinaris' "mindless" christology (the
pun is Gregory's) was precisely the danger
that we might not be saved in all our constituent parts. If the incarnation was to effect
an abiding cure for the universal disease of
our fallen condition, then it must be more
than just a sarkōsis, the Johannine kai ho
Logos sarx egeneto notwithstanding. As Athanasius before him, Gregory saw the term sarx
in this passage as standing for the whole man,
and therefore enanthrōpēsis (enmanment) might
be a more exact term than sarkōsis (incarnation).[3] The well-known dictum that "Quod assumptum non est non sanatum," though certainly not original with Gregory, does express
his view with some degree of accuracy.[4]

---

1. Ep. 101 (PG 37.184B).
2. Ep. ad Diocaes., in H. Lietzmann, Apollinaris von Laodicea und seine Schule (Tübingen, 1904), p. 256. Cf. R. A. Norris, Manhood
and Christ (Oxford, 1963), p. 119.
3. Ep. 101 (PG 37.189A).
4. Ibid. (PG 37.181C-184A). This idea ap-

Gregory's triadological thought steers, as we have seen, a middle course between two extremes. Against Sabellianism, he affirms the individuated hypostasis of the Son in distinct relation to the Father; against Arianism, he asserts the full divinity of the Son as a result of his equal and coëternal participation in the ousia of the Godhead. And when he turns to christology proper (i.e., the relation between the human and divine "natures" in the incarnate Son), he argues, against the Apollinarians, for the fullness of the human nature assumed by the Logos in the incarnation. But when Gregory goes beyond "proclamation" and tries his hand at "explanation," he is fully aware of the ultimate inadequacy of his words. When faced with the question of how two natures (physeis) can meet in one Person (hypostasis), Gregory's conceptual framework is such that he is unable finally to provide a satisfactory explanation. Yet we must avoid the temptation of evaluating Gregory's language here from a point of view informed by christological developments which had not yet taken place. Much of what he says, for instance, could be pilloried as crypto-Nestorian; more, perhaps, could be described as quasi-Eutychian. But, if we avoid a "post-judicial" approach to Gregory's shortcomings, we soon discover that he himself is aware of them and forced finally to stand mute before the "divine mystery." Yet this in no way

---

pears earlier in Tertullian, De Carne Christi, 10, and in Origen, Dial. c. Heracl., 6.20-7.5. See A. Grillmeier, "Quod non est assumptum," LTK, 8, pp. 954-6. M. F. Wiles has written provocatively on this subject; see his "Soteriological Arguments in the Fathers," SP, 9 (Texte und Untersuchungen, 94; Berlin, 1966), pp. 321-5, and "The Unassumed in the Unhealed," RS, 4 (1969), pp. 47-56.

diminishes Gregory's undertaking the responsibility both to understand and to proclaim, in spite of the unsettled christological terminology of his day.[1]

Gregory's most constructive and positive contribution to this problem is undoubtedly his application of what were trinitarian categories to the formula of the two-fold constitution of the God-man in Christ. The distinction within the Godhead between Father and Son, he says, is one of "Person" (allos kai allos). The distinction within the incarnate Logos, however, between the humanity and divinity, is one of "nature" (allo kai allo).[2] This latter distinction, he says elsewhere (anticipating Cyril of Alexandria's arguments against Nestorius), is possible only "in thought" (diistantai tais epinoiais).[3] Neither of the two natures, although the one is fully God and the other fully man, can be hypostasized; although Christ is of a "double" or "two-fold" constitution, there is but one hypostasis to the incarnate Logos.[4]

In spite of this constant emphasis on the unity of the Person of Christ, Gregory still feels constrained to explain further how such a unity is possible, and in so doing ranges over a wide field of terminological formulas. It is not surprising, therefore, that, in using so vast an array of concepts, much of

---

1. Mason (op. cit., pp. xvi ff) makes a point of warning the reader of the christological "dangers" inherent in much of Gregory's terminology in the Theological Orations. Cf. Barbel, op. cit., pp. 162ff, and A. Grillmeier, Christ in Christian Tradition (New York, 1964), pp. 280f.
2. Ep. 101 (PG 37.180A).
3. Or. 30.8 (PG 36.113B).
4. Or. 38.15 (PG 36.328C).

what he says is inconsistent, and sometimes
blatantly contradictory. In his correspondence
with Cledonius concerning the Apollinarian
controversy, Gregory insists adamantly on the
reality of the complete union between God and
man in Christ; there cannot be, he says, "two
Sons," or "two Gods," or two Persons."[1] And the
terms he uses to express this divine-human
union, such as krasis, sugkrasis, and mixis,
indicate, if not an appreciation of how such
terms would later become suspect, at least a
desire to "keep trying."[2] Anticipating a phrase
used later by Augustine, Gregory suggests that
the distinction between the two "natures" can
be understood if we think of the divine as
"without a mother," and of the human as "without a father,"[3] although later he will recognize the difficulties inherent in such a statement.[4] And, reflecting Origen, Gregory claims
that the union between God and humanity is
effected by means of a mediatorial nous or
psychē, because the mind (or soul) has a natural
affinity to both the divine and human natures in
Christ.[5] In a poem entitled, "On the Incarnation,
Against Apollinaris," he puts it in this fashion:

> For since God cannot be mixed with
>   flesh,

---

1. Ep. 101 and 102 (PG 37.180A, 196A).
2. Cf. Kelly, op. cit., p. 298. For a
study of these and related terms as employed in
the writings of the Fathers and seen against
their philosophical background, see H. A.
Wolfson, The Philosophy of the Church Fathers,
2nd ed. (Cambridge, Mass., 1964), pp. 364ff.
3. Or. 38.2 (PG 35.313AB); cf. Or. 30.21
(PG 36.132B) and Augustine, Trac. in Joan., 8.
4. See Ep. 101 (PG 37.180A).
5. Or. 2.23 (PG 35.432C-433A) and Or.
29.19 (PG 36.100A); cf. Origen, De Princ., 2.6.3.

His soul and mind were intermediary
  as it were:
His soul as the spouse of the flesh;
  His mind as God's
Own image. Thus the divine nature was
  mated
With its kin, and had communion with
  the flesh;
Thus both divinizing and deified
  were God.[1]

Again, in Aristotelian manner, Gregory
asserts the union of natures to have been
achieved because the divine nature "prevailed"
over the human.[2] He also resorts to the familiar analogy which compares the christological
union to the inseparable union of body and soul
in man, unaware, perhaps, that this had been
one of Apollinaris' favorite formulas.[3]
    To discuss Gregory's several christological
concepts in abstracto, however, is to fail to
uncover the ultimate soteriological environment
in which, for him, they operate. We have seen
that the incarnation, as Gregory views it, had
salvation as its sole motive; therefore the
incarnate Logos must be God. We have also

---

1. 1.1.10.56-61 (PG 37.469). This translation was made by Herbert Musurillo and appears
in his soon to be published article, "God and
Man in the Poetry of Gregory of Nazianzus." I
am grateful to Professor Musurillo for letting
me have a copy.
    2. Or. 29.19 (PG 36.100A).
    3. Ep. 101 (PG 37.180A). Cf. Apollinaris,
De unione, 5, and Fragments 129 and 148 in
Litzmann (op. cit.), pp. 187, 239, and 247.
On this problem, see M. F. Wiles, "Psychological Analogies in the Fathers," SP, 11 (Teste
und Untersuchungen, 108; Berlin, 1972), pp.
264-7.

seen that the incarnation had the salvation
of mankind as its controlling purpose; therefore the incarnate Son of God must be fully
human. But more than this, the incarnation is
the means whereby our ultimate union with God
is effected; therefore, the union of natures
in Christ--however inadequately expressed--
must be a real henōsis, and not merely a "partnership." It must, accordingly, be a union
that at one and the same time allows for the
distinction between Creator and creature as
well as pointing to a single subject of the
divine oikonomia.

As Gregory understands it, the incarnation
was the assumption by God of human nature with
the express purpose of restoring to humankind
the originally intended theōsis which was the
goal of its Godward pilgrimage. And precisely
in the Person of Jesus Christ is this theōsis
effected. For this reason Gregory can claim
that the incarnate Logos is both "flesh-bear-
ing God" and "God-bearing man."[1] Christ, who
is the Second Adam, bears in himself all of
human nature, i.e., "all that I am," so that
we may fully partake of him through this
union.[2] We find therefore, and not unexpected-
ly, that throughout all of Gregory's writings
there runs, as it were, the "figured bass" of
theōsis, supporting the intermingling "counter-
point" by which he attempts to express his
christological concerns. A. Grillmeier is one
of the few historians to have pointed to the
full implications of this in his statement
that the "divinization of Christ's human nature" serves as the theological foundation

---

1. Ep. 102 (PG 37.200B). To assert the
former without the latter would be to fall
into the dangers of Apollinarianism, and for
this reason Gregory insists on both.
2. Or. 31.1, 6 (PG 36.104C, 109C).

86

for the concept of the "divinization of man."[1]
The unity of Christ's Person, for Gregory, is
theōsis. It is a theōsis of Christ's human nature, not because this human nature was "repentant" or because it "improved," but because when it was joined to God, it became
God; the higher nature of this intimate union
"prevailed."[2] Or, as Gregory says elsewhere,
the human nature of Christ was "sanctified" by
the mere presence (parousia) of the divine,
not by an action of operation (energeia) on
the part of the divine.[3] No element of Christ's
human nature can be opposed to the divine,
since the "whole of it is deified."[4] In different terms, Christ is of two natures, spirit and
flesh; the former deifies and the latter is
deified (τὸ μὲν ἐθέωσε, τὸ δὲ ἐθεώθη).[5] Or,
using still different anthropological terms,
Gregory says that the body (soma) of Christ
became God by virtue of theōsis (τῇ θεώσει
θεόſ).[6] That which the Godhead assumed, he explains, was "anointed with divinity" and became "equal to God" (ὁμόθεον).[7] Or, more precisely, "The two natures of Christ are one
by the union, God becoming man and man becoming God."[8]

It is impossible, therefore, to avoid the
conclusion that Gregory's soteriologically
oriented christology is centered upon his concept of theōsis. "In the incarnation of the

---

1. Grillmeier, op. cit., p. 283.
2. Or. 25.16 (PG 35.1221B) and Or. 29.19
(PG 36.100A).
3. Or. 30.21 (PG 36.132B).
4. Ibid., 12 (PG 35.117C).
5. Or. 38.13 (PG 36.325BC); see also 1.1.
10.61 (PG 37.469).
6. Or. 39.16 (PG 36.353B).
7. Or. 45.13 (PG 36.641A).
8. Ep. 101 (PG 37.180A).

Son, human nature was not only anointed with
a superabundant overflowing of grace, but was
assumed into an intimate and hypostatical
unity with God himself."[1] And, most important,
the theōsis of Christ's humanity is, for Gregory, the paradigm of the theōsis of all humanity. It is the fundamental postulate upon
which rests the whole unfolding "work" of
Christ. What Christ achieves in his God-man-
hood is not the work of a spiritualized or
"adopted" humanity, but the work of the "humanity of God."[2] The theōsis of Christ's human nature is not the disappearance of his
humanity, or the total absorption of the lower
into the higher, or even some kind of metaphysical "transubstantiation"; rather, it is the
participation of the human nature in the divine, a participation so complete, so intimate
and interpenetrating, that to call the "deified"
human nature "God" is not a semantic trick
but a description of reality.[3]
   In spite of Gregory's predominant stress
on theōsis as that term which best renders in-
telligible the nature and purpose of the incarnation, and more particularly, the mode of
the christological union, it would be misleading to conclude that he holds a "physical"
view of salvation, thereby belonging to that
school of Greek Fathers who have so often and
by so many been accused of holding to a theory

   1. So Georges Florovsky, "The Lamb of God,"
SJT, 4 (1951), p. 17; repeated verbatim in "The
Resurrection of Life," BHDS, 48 (Apr., 1959), p.
14.2. Or. 45.22 (PG 36.653B).
   2. Or. 45.22 (PG 36.653B).
   3. See Georges Florovsky, Eastern Fathers
of the Fourth Century (Paris, 1931), p. 116,
and also Plagnieux, op. cit., pp. 183ff.

of "salvation by incarnation," i.e., that the
salvation of mankind was wrought solely in and
by the incarnation.[1] To a certain extent, of
course, his concept of salvation is physical.
The incarnation effected a theōsis of human nature, spiritual and physical, and it is this
theōsis that becomes the font of our salvation, because, as we noted above, the incarnation had to involve the assumption by God of
human nature in its physical and spiritual totality. And the incarnation was the new creation
that was the stronger "medicine" for the fallen;
it was an "innovation" made in the created order,
and the means whereby the laws of (fallen) nature were upset, and our whole nature "remodel-
led."[2]

---

1. There has been a considerable amount of
controversy on this issue, even to this day.
Harnack (DG, 3, pp. 165ff) is the first major
historian to interpret the Greek Fathers in
this fashion. His thesis, however, has often
been challenged. See, for instance, Gross, op.
cit., pp. 248f and 347; Aubineau, op. cit.,
p. 39; R. Seeberg, Text-Book of the History of
Doctrine, trans., C. E. Hay (Grand Rapids,
1969), pp. 297ff; H. Chadwick, Early Christian
Thought and the Classical Tradition (London,
1966), pp. 92ff; J. Pelikan, The Christian
Tradition, 1: The Emergence of the Catholic
Tradition (Chicago, 1971), passim; but cf.
Festugière, op. cit., p. 99 .
2. Or. 38.2 (PG 36.313B) and Ep. 202 (PG
37.332B). J. Daniélou has said that Gregory's
concept of the work of Christ "represents an
overthrow of the natural order of things resulting from the revelation of a reality absolutely new and unforeseeable." The Angels
and their Mission (Westminster, 1957), pp. 41f.

To this extent, then, but to this extent
only, Gregory can be said to hold a view that
equates salvation (or theōsis) with the incarnation. Time and again we find passages where
he asserts that the enanthrōpēsis of the Son
of God was the very means by which the "cure"
for mankind's disease was effected.[1] Yet, for
all this, we cannot assume that the incarnation was either "physical" (since we have already seen its "spiritual" dimensions) or that
the incarnation was the "final act" in the divine drama of salvation. The incarnation, in
fact, is but a part of the divine oikonomia,
and is to fallen mankind what creation was to
Adam and Eve, i.e., just a beginning. The incarnation, according to Gregory, is not only
the salvific assumption of human nature; it
is also the entrance of God into human life.
The incarnation is the "birth" of God into
the midst of everything that it means to be
human. It is the assumption, not only of the
whole of human nature, but, with it, everything that belongs to human nature, i.e., the
condition of humanity as well as the whole
of human life.[2] Just as Gregory's descrip-

---

1. Or. 30.2 (PG 36.105B); Or. 34.10 (PG 36.
252A); Or. 38.3, 13 (PG 35.313A, 325BC). Lot-
Borodine (op. cit., pp. 34f) writes that, for
the Greek Fathers, "l'incarnation est déjà une
Rédemption, car ce que le Christ a assumé, il
le rédime." But she goes on to say that this
reparatio is the "condition première de la glo-
rificatio." See also Gross' statement (op. cit.,
p. 248): "L'incarnation est une cause éloignée
de la Rédemption, en tant qu'elle permet au
Sauveur de donner en raçon corps pour corps,
âme pour âme; le salut lui-même est dès lors
directement réalisé par la passion et la mort
de Christ."
2. Or. 26.6 (PG 35.1235BC), Or. 30.6 (PG
36.109C). See Spidlik, op. cit., p. 109.

tion of primitive anthropology centered much
less on a static definition of a person's
constituent parts as created than on the dynamic purpose for which we were created, so too
his incarnational views would be sadly misinterpreted were we to be satisfied merely with
a description of the christological union itself. The "mechanics" of such a union are indeed important, but more important for Gregory,
are the life and work of him who is the product
of that union, Jesus the incarnate Son. So
again we find that Gregory's thought operates
more effectively in the realm of dynamic function than in that of static description. Which
is to say, what the incarnate Logos does must
go hand in hand with who the incarnate Logos
is. And what he does, claims Gregory, is effective for our salvation precisely because of the
"power of the incarnation."[1]

In his very first Oration Gregory exhorts
his congregation with these words: "Let us become like Christ, since Christ became like us;
let us become gods for his sake, since he for
ours became man."[2] This remarkable exhortation
is clear evidence that Gregory in no way believes salvation to have been completely accomplished in the act of incarnation. His
saying "let us become" instead of "we have become" indicates that, for mankind, salvation
has yet to be worked out; the incarnation has
effected our redemption, but only potentially. Salvation, in a word, embraces more than
the salvific assumption of human nature. The
double metathesis that occurs in Christ's enanthrōpēsis is not restricted solely to the

---

1. Ibid., 14 (PG 36.121C).
2. Or. 1.5 (PG 35.397C). Was it a typogra-
phical error or an unconscious distrust of the
vocabulary of theōsis which led the NPNF to
translate θεοί in this passage as "God's"?

91

theo-anthropological exchange of properties.[1]
One has only to examine Gregory's interpretation of a further kind of exchange of properties to realize this, e.g., Christ's poverty
is the means whereby we are made rich, his
servitude the means whereby we are made free,
his temptation the instrument whereby we might
overcome temptation.[2]

Theōsis has occurred in the incarnation,
but only the theōsis of Christ's human nature.
The restoration to us of theōsis as the ultimate goal of human growth, however, is neither
immediate nor automatic. Georges Florovsky, in
another context, has expressed this well:
" The incarnation was not just a metaphysical
miracle, it was the mystery of the Love divine,
of the Divine identification with the lost
man . . . God was not manifest in the flesh in
order to recreate the fallen world at once by
the exercise of His omnipotent might . . ."[3]
Our restoration, for Gregory, began in the
assumption by God of our human nature, and
then continued in his total identification
with our human life. Gregory portrays this restoration of human nature and life in many
ways, but a few recurring themes stand out
above the others.

Perhaps the most prevalent theme describing
the incarnate life found in Gregory's writings
is that of condescension. The Son of God's
assumption of "all of me" (nature) and "all of
mine" (life) was, if we may use a spatial metaphor, a "coming down." God came down that we
might go up. God in Christ condescended not
just to the static attributes of the human
constitution but also to the ongoing conditions

---

1. See Or. 2.24 (PG 35.433A).
2. Or. 1.5 (PG 35.397C-400A); also Or. 30.6
(PG 36.112A) and Or. 43.61 (PG 36.576B).
3. Florovsky, "The Lamb of God," pp. 17-8.

of our existence. He condescended to human
hunger that we might be fed, to human thirst
that we might drink our fill, to human weariness that we might find rest, to human tears
that we might cry no more.[1] And, says Gregory,
our appropriation of these gifts bestowed upon
us by the condescension of the incarnate Logos
consists of our ascension: he "came down" and
"became man" that we might "go up" and "become
God."[2]

Yet it would seem that, for all his emphasis on the condescension of the incarnate life,
Gregory, like the majority of Greek Fathers,
does not want God to "come down" too far. He
is obviously anxious to safeguard the Deity
from human suffering, to affirm the almost unassailable assertion of divine impassibility.
In reviewing the Gospel portrait of Jesus, he
refuses, at first, to allow the so-called "human acts" of Jesus to be assigned to the incarnate Son's "higher nature."[3] He will stress
the condescension of the Son, but at the same
time is loath to attribute to "him who assumed our nature" properties which he feels are
more appropriate to the "nature assumed."
Particularly in the Theological Orations is
this division between "divine" and "human"
acts noticeable. The Arians, who were only
too quick to point out the very "un-godlike"

---

1. Or. 29.20 (PG 36.100C-101C); cf. Or.
37.2 (PG 36.284C), where sleep, weariness,
tears, and the like, are not removed but
"hallowed."
2. Or. 30.21 (PG 36.133A).
3. Athanasius had the same difficulties
in combatting his Arian opponents' agile use
of "proof-texts."
4. Here is a case in point where the interpreter might be tempted (anachronistically)
to accuse Gregory of Nestorianism.

qualities in Jesus Christ, were the prime target of the Orations, and Gregory answers them by saying (an approach not original with him but a standard part of the Nicene arsenal): "What is lofty, you are to apply to the Godhead . . . and what is lowly to his composite nature (synthetos)."[1] In the same manner, Gregory seems to be somewhat embarassed by the Son's apparent "ignorance and growth" as reported in Luke 2:52, and attempts to explain them away by arguing that the real "stature" of the incarnate Son is only gradually disclosed, but was never less, in fact, than what was finally disclosed (a kind of "revelatory docetism," if you will).[2]

Not until the years of his retirement does Gregory come to terms with the difficulties inherent in such a double portrait of Jesus, and then only because he is forced to by his Apollinarian opponents.[3] Here he will finally abandon his previous approach, as extorted from him by the Arians, and assert a single subject behind all of the acts of Jesus. He will dismiss as "wanting in reason" the kind

---

1. Or. 29.18 (PG 36.97BC). It is not clear whether, by this "synthesis," Gregory means the union of God and man or is referring solely to Christ's human nature, since man, too, as we have seen, is of a composite nature. See similar statements in Or. 29.20 (PG 100C-101C) and Or. 30.1, 15 (PG 36.104C, 124AB).

2. Or. 43.38 (PG 36.354BC); see also Or. 29.18 (PG 36.97AB).

3. Gregory does not admit, however, that he is here repudiating a view which he himself had held earlier. It is hard to believe that he forgot. On the implications of this apparent contradiction, see my "Christology and Exegesis in the Cappadocians," CH, 40 (1971), pp. 389-96.

of thinking that assigns the words "Where
have you laid Lazarus?" (because this shows
ignorance) to the anthrōpinos of Christ.
while assigning the words "Lazarus, come
forth!" (because this is a "miracle") to his
theotēs.[1] It is not until later in life, then,
after a shift of theological opponents had
taken place, that Gregory no longer so "di-
vides the things of Christ."[2] But, throughout, in spite of these difficulties and con-
tradictions, Gregory's abiding stress on the
condescension of the incarnate life remains a
major theme in his writings.

A second and parallel theme by which Gregory seeks to interpret the divine life, that
of kenosis or divine self-emptying, also
stands out prominently. Here, too, Gregory wa-
vers somewhat in the face of the Gospel evidence, but there is no question as to his conviction that the well-known passage from Phil-
ippians 2:7 is more than just an apt metaphor.
At first, Gregory will claim that, in the incarnate life, the Son of God "continued to be
what he was, and what he was not, that he assumed."[3] But later he will balance this statement with the assertion that the Son of God
"put aside what he was and assumed what he was
not" (ὃ ἦν ἐκένωσε καὶ ὃ μὴ ἦν προσέλαβεν).[4]
By such a self emptying, however, the incarnate
Son's deity is not lessened; he did not become
two, but one out of two (two φύσειϛ not two
υἱοί), and both that which assumed and that
which was assumed are God.[5]

Just as the divine condescension was ef-

---

1. Ep. 102 (PG 37.201A) with reference to
John 11:34, 43. Cf. Or. 29.20 (PG 36.101A).
2. Ep. 102 (PG 37.201A).
3. Or. 29.18 (PG 36.100A).
4. Or. 37.2 (PG 36.248C).
5. Ibid. See also Or. 2.23 (PG 35.432BC).

fected for the salvation of man, so too with the divine self-emptying: he that is full empties himself (κενοῦται) of his glory (δόξα) so that "I may share in his fulness."[1] Or, to use Florovsky's apt phrase, the divine "kenosis" was "no reduction of Christ's divinity . . . it was, on the contrary, a lifting up of man, the sanctification or 'deification' of human nature, the theōsis."[2] It is well to remember, however, that for Gregory this divine self-emptying is only "temporary"; within the dimensions of the oikonomia of God, the kenosis of God ends when the purposes for which God became man are ultimately achieved.[3]

Parallel to the ideas of condescension and kenosis there is a third theme by which Gregory articulates his view of the incarnate life, the familiar theme of "recapitulation." Christ, who is Second Adam, recapitulates the life of the first Adam. The new is substituted for the old; the old is resumed in the new. The incarnate Son exchanges his restorative properties for our diseased attributes. The history of Adam and his seed is re-lived in the history of the Son of God on earth: the Virgin is Eve, the manger is the Garden, and all that happened before happens again, re-storatively, in Christ.[4] "In himself," says Gregory, "Christ sums up and contains all that is."[5] And, more important, in him the Archetype of the faded image in us represented, re-established, and re-impressed (potentially) upon mankind as that very quality in us by which our Godward progress can once more become a realistic and ultimately real vocation.[6]

---

1. Or. 38.13 (PG 36.325C).
2. Florovsky, "The Lamb of God," p. 19.
3. Or. 38.13 (PG 36.325C).
4. Or. 2.23-4 (PG 35.433AB).
5. Or. 38.7 (PG 36.317B).
6. See 1.1.10.20-1 (PG 37.467).

These themes of condescension, self-emptying, and recapitulation are, we conclude, three
common modes by which Gregory indicates the
salvific power of the incarnate life. The three,
needless to say, cannot be separated from each
other, nor is Gregory's portrait of Christ restricted solely to them; they are inter-related
and mutually interdependent parts of a far wider
picture. Nor, of course, are these themes original with Gregory, each of them having deep roots
within the scriptural, sub-apostolic, and early
patristic tradition. But in Gregory's hand they
merge together to give a striking portrayal of
the oikonomia of the divine Logos. The incarnation is the assumption by the divine of all that
is human, human nature and human life. God con-
descends both to become man and to live as man.
In so doing, he puts aside his "glory" so as to
limit it to human dimensions, knowing that "humility is the best road to exaltation."[1] And in
his person he recapitulates all that we are and
have been so that what we are to be becomes more
than a pious hope or sought-after promise, but
the truest thing that can be said of us.

But there is one more barrier that stands
between us and the resumption of our progress
towards theōsis. We have sinned, and in sinning
have brought mortality into the human situation.
Therefore, the ultimate meaning of the incarnation is to be found, not only in the divine assumption of human nature, or of human life, but
also in the divine assumption of human death itself. "The climax of the Incarnate Life is the
Cross,"[2] and it is to Gregory's contribution to
our understanding of this event within the divine oikonomia that we now turn.

---

1. Or. 38.7 (PG 36.317B).
2. So Florovsky, "The Lamb of God," p. 18.

CHAPTER V -- THE ECONOMY OF THE BODY OF CHRIST

Part Two -- Death

The Cross of Jesus Christ is, for Gregory, the culmination and fulfillment of the oikono- mia of the incarnation. It is the prime instru- ment of salvation. Gregory sees made manifest on the Cross of Calvary the deeper meaning of the condescension and self-emptying of the Son of God, and of his recapitulation of the whole created order. God comes down--all the way down--to the lowest level of our fallen con- dition, namely death.[1] God empties himself of his glory and humbles himself before the altar of divine sacrificial love.[2] And God resumes in himself the misdirected pilgrimage of the first Adam, thereby obliterating on the Tree of the Cross the consequences of the viola- tion of the Tree of Knowledge so that we might once more partake of the Tree of Life.[3]

In Gregory's constant struggle with the Arians, nowhere does he show less patience with their views than when they claim that the Cross of Christ represents the ultimate in di- vine folly, if indeed Christ be God. At one time he even goes so far as to say that Christ died in vain for such "unthankful creatures" (i.e., the Arians), only to add a little later: "Oh! that Christ would give his life for you who, because of your kakodoxia, are dead!"[4]

---

1. Or. 29.20 (PG 36.100C-101C) and Or. 37.2 (PG 36.284C).

2. See Or. 37.3 (PG 36.285B).

3. Or. 2.25 (PG 35.433C), Or. 29.20 (PG 36. 101B) and Or. 33.9 (PG 36.225C).

4. Or. 38.14 (PG 36.328A, 329C).

The Arians, according to Gregory, argue that
for the Good Shepherd to lay down his life for
the sheep is to compromise the ungenerate and
impassible nature of God and to insult his infinite majesty, if indeed the "Good Shepherd"
is consubstantial with the Father.[1] Gregory is
filled with "anger and grief" when he hears
such words, for he believes the Arian view ultimately dishonors Christ precisely on account
of that which should bring him most honor,
namely, his suffering ana death.[2] They refuse
to realize, he says, that the humility of
Christ is the very principle of his exaltation.[3] But, let the Jews be offended, let the
Greeks laugh,[4] and let the heretics talk until
their tongues ache;[5] it is still the Passion
of Christ that "justifies us" and provides for
our "return to God."[6]

Whether arguing against the "heretics" or
preaching before the "faithful" (activities
which were often simultaneous for Gregory), his
stress on the Cross as the means whereby mankind is saved stems from his insistence that
the whole person be saved, including the sin
that caused the fall and the mortality which
resulted from it. In the incarnation, the assumption of human nature was complete; in the
incarnate life, the assumption of human existence was complete, with one exception: sin.[7]
Yet, says Gregory, for us Christ was "made
sin" and took that sin with him and nailed it

1. Ibid. See also Or. 29.18 (PG 36.97B).
2. Or. 37.4 (PG 36.285C).
3. Or. 38.14 (PG 36.328B).
4. An allusion to 1 Cor. 1:23.
5. Or. 38.2 (PG 36.313B).
6. Ibid., 4 (PG 36.316AB).
7. Or. 30.21 (PG 36132B), Or. 37.1 (PG 36.
284A), Or. 38.12 (PG 36.325B), and Or. 45.13
(PG 36.641B).

to the cross.[1] So, too, Christ became a "curse" for us, and thereby destroyed the "curse" laid upon mankind.[2] But one enemy was left: death. So Christ's assumption of human death was complete, except, as Gregory explains, the grave could not hold him. Accordingly, in Christ's death, death itself was conquered.[3]

Yet, parallel to Gregory's hesitation to have Christ come down too far into our passible condition is his hesitation to have "sin," the "curse," and "death" itself too closely identified with the Savior's Person; it is easier for Gregory to speak of such things within the mode of Christ's being. And to this extent he reflects the predominant strain of thought concerning Christ's death as represented by the majority of the Greek Fathers. One example will suffice to indicate this hesitation:

> Christ becomes all things to all men
> so that he may gain them all . . .
> He becomes even sin itself and a
> very curse, not that he is in fact
> either of these but is referred to
> as such. For how could he be sin,
> he who sets us free from sin, or how
> could he be a curse, he who redeems
> us from the curse of the law?[4]

But in spite of these characteristic caveats, Gregory still insists on the centrality of the Cross as the climax to the divine oikono-mia, and, as we shall see, describes it in terms that go far beyond many patristic au-

---

1. Or. 43.64 (PG 36.581A).
2. Or. 2.55 (PG 35.465B), Or. 30.5 (PG 36.108C), and Ep. 101 (PG 37.190C).
3. Or 29.20 (PG 36.101B).
4. Or. 37.1 (PG 36.284A).

thors in the deep sense of reality they portray. The assumption of human nature in the incarnation elicits from Gregory the statement
that "little Bethlehem" has led us "back to
Paradise."[1] The consequent assumption of human
life and death draws from him the assertion
that "a few drops of blood recreate the whole
world."[2] By the Cross of Christ, the sting of
death has been abolished and victory over the
grave established.[3] "Coming down" as a servant,
Christ "went up" to the Cross, "carrying my
sins with him."[4] "Representing us in his own
Person, Christ made our folly and sins his
own,"[5] and when he was crucified, "he crucified
my sins" at the same time.[6] The incarnate Son
died on the Cross, and by so doing he destroyed
death and gave us life.[7]

As is already apparent, nowhere is Gregory's
language more deeply rooted in the New Testament
than when he is describing the Cross of Jesus
Christ; his writings abound with scriptural
metaphors and concepts. Yet he uses these metaphors and concepts, not in slavish mimicry of
New Testament texts, but in such a way as to
make them his own and to mold them into a pattern that best expresses his own convictions
as to the glory of Calvary. The biblical image
which he most often calls upon is that which
represents Christ's death as a sacrifice.[8]
In the sacrifice on the Cross, Christ is both
the offerer and the one who is offered, both

---

1. Or. 38.17 (PG 36.329D-332A).
2. Or. 45.29 (PG 36.664A).
3. Ibid., 22 (PG 36.653C).
4. Or. 4.78 (PG 35.604BC).
5. Or. 30.5 (PG 36.109B).
6. Or. 38.16 (PG 36.329C).
7. Or. 29.20 (PG 36.101B).
8. Gregory uses both thuma and thusia, but
his preference is for the latter.

the High Priest and the Lamb. Prefigured in
the Old Testament, the sacrifice of Calvary
does not abolish the Jewish concept of sacrifice; rather, it sanctifies all past sacrifices since Christ is the one true willing
sacrifice who, by his voluntary obedience,
cleanses and purifies the whole world.[1]

It is in this concept of Christ as both
Priest and Victim that Gregory exhibits the
greatest precision of thought concerning the
problem of the two natures of Christ. In his
description of the incarnate life, as we have
seen, Gregory vacillates between several posi-
tions; while always insisting that the Person
of the incarnate Son is one, he nevertheless
often resorts to explaining Christ's "human"
activities by ascribing them to the "lower
nature," and his "divine" activities by ascribing them to his "higher nature," only to repu-
diate such a view in his later writings. But
in Gregory's treatment of the passion and death
of Christ he is considerably more consistent,
and, here more than anywhere else, asserts
what we can call a true περιχώρησιϛ of natures.[2]
(Gregory, as Stephan has pointed out,[3] is the
first Greek Father to apply this term to the
christological union.) The obvious reason for

---

1. Or. 1.7 (PG 35.400C), Or. 2.88 (PG 35.
492B), Or. 12.2 (PG 35.845A), Or. 30.6, 21 (PG
36.109C, 132C), Or. 37.4 (PG 36.288A), Or. 38.
16 (PG 36.329C), and Or. 45.13 (PG 36.640C).

2. Ep. 101 (PG 37.181C).

3. Stephan, op. cit., p. 16. G. L. Prestige, however, has said that Gregory's use of this
term, in the context in which it appears, is
not specifically directed to the natures of
Christ; it refers, rather, to the "titles" of
Christ. "Περιχωρέω and περιχώρησιϛ in the
Fathers," JTS, 19, No. 115 (Apr., 1928), pp.
242f.

such an assertion of the completeness of the
God-man union in Christ is that our whole
nature--body, soul, and mind--has been effected by death.[1] Further, since victory over death
is an undertaking possible only to God, the
passion of the incarnate Son must in fact be
the action of God, i.e., of the one hypostasis
of the two conjoined natures. There are some,
says Gregory (directing his remarks against the
crypto-docetism inherent in much of hellenic
thought), who think that the theōtes of Christ
withdrew from the union before the time of the
passion, as if it were afraid of suffering.
But, he counters, it is precisely on the Cross
where the salvific activity of God is made most
manifest, for it is here that we are saved by
the sufferings of him who could not suffer.[2]

Gregory is treading a very narrow path
here, given the world of thought in which he
was nurtured. He denies, on the one hand, that
the divine nature of Christ was put to death,
or that Christ suffered "in his own divinity,"
asserting that the incarnate Son was passible
in flesh, but impassible in his Godhead (παθη-
τὸν σαρκὶ, ἀπαθῆ θεότητι).[3] What Christ suffered, in other words, he suffered ὣς ἄνθρωπος.[4]
But such phrases occur in Gregory's writing
only when the context demands that he make a
distinction--as such a distinction, for him,
must be made--between the two natures of the

---

1. See Or. 30.21 (PG 36.132B).
2. Ibid., 5 (PG 36.109S). Gregory does not
identify these "docetics" by name, but possibly he is referring to one of the views of
Valentinian gnosticism, whose terminology and
doctrines were familiar to him. See Irenaeus,
Adv. haer., 1.30.13.
3. Ep. 101 (PG 37.177B) and Ep. 202 (PG
37.333A).
4. Or. 30.14 (PG 36.124A).

incarnate Son. And, as we have noted, such a distinction is possible only in thought. His more normal way of speaking, however, when attempting to delineate the meaning of the sacrifice of the Cross, is to refer, not to the "natures" of Christ, but to the one Person of the incarnate Son of God. And here we find him speaking very unambiguously of the Second Adam as θεὸς παθητός [1] a phrase which at first glance seems strange coming from the pen of an Easterner. One historian has labelled it a "daring oxymoron,"[2] while the great Migne felt constrained to warn his readers that "humana Christi natura hic intelligitur."[3] Yet Gregory without a doubt uses such language intentionally. That which is impassible, he says, is "mingled with suffering."[4] Or, again, he speaks of the church as that body called together by the "great sufferings of God for us."[5] In our fallen, sinful, and mortal condition, he says elsewhere, we "needed an incarnate God, a God put to death."[6] Though superior to suffering, God is "crucified."[7] It is the "blood of God, his passion and his death," says Gregory, that are our hope for salvation.[8]

When speaking of the death of Christ, then, Gregory stresses with a terminological boldness unequalled by any of his predecessors (with the possible exception of Ignatius and

---

1. Ibid., 1 (PG 36.104C). On the implications of terms such as these, see F. M. Young, "A Reconsideration of Alexandrian Christology," JEH, 22 (1971), pp. 103-14.
2. A. J. Mason, op. cit., loc. cit.
3. PG 36.104, n. 56.
4. Or 39.13 (PG 36.349A).
5. Or. 21.24 (PG 35.1109A).
6. Or. 45.28 (PG 36.661C).
7. Or. 43.64 (PG 36.581A).
8. Or. 45.19 (PG 36.649C).

Melito) the unity of the hypostasis of the incarnate Son. Gregory is not unaware of this boldness, and often comments himself upon it, admitting that such language may be confusing to some, yet insisting that he speaks thus of necessity in order to combat the adversaries of the church.[1] Karl Holl has remarked, in reflecting upon Gregory's use of the term "suffering God," that the Theologian takes no delight in naked paradox for its own sake; rather, his formulations here reveal an uncommon but valid attempt to probe deeper than ever before into the mystery of salvation.[2] Yet, in spite of the various interpretations that have been made (and doubtless will continue to be made), Gregory's point is quite simple. Jesus Christ is the union of God and man; he is the conjoining of two natures, divine and human, the latter of which is deified by the former. God becomes man. And man "becomes God" in Jesus Christ. If, then, it is possible to speak of Christ "dying in his human nature," it is equally possible--and, for Gregory, more

---

1. Ibid.
2. Holl. op. cit., p. 180. Barbel (op. cit., pp. 170ff), on the other hand, interprets Gregory's language here more or less in terms of the Chalcedonian Symbol of 451, while Florovsky ("Lamb of God," pp. 24-5) suggests that Gregory can best be understood by reference to a formula that is more from John of Damascus than from Gregory himself: ". . . the Person, who was crucified and died, was divine--there was no human hypostasis in Christ. . . The main point is that it was a death within the Hypostasis of the Word, the death of 'enhypostasized' humanity." Cf. John of Damascus, Exp. fidei orth., 3.15. See also J. Chéné's helpful article, "Unus de Trinitate passus est," RSR, 53 (1965), pp. 545-88.

pertinent--to speak of the "death and crucifixion of God."[1] Christ, says Gregory, was the
perfect victim, "not on account of his deity
alone (than which nothing can be more perfect),
but also because the assumed nature was
anointed with deity and became that by which
it was anointed."[2]

If Gregory makes extensive use of the biblical concept of the death of Christ as a
sacrifice, adding to it his own special emphasis on the passio of the one incarnate Word,
he pays less attention to the New Testament
concept of the Cross as the instrument by which
the Devil was overcome. Only in two short passages does he refer to the defeat of Satan at
the hands of the crucified Christ, each time
making use of that image so popular among the
Fathers, the image of the "deceit of the Devil."[3] This image was to gain wider popularity
through Gregory of Nyssa's "fish-hook" theory
and Augustine's "mousetrap" theory, but already by the time of Origen it had found its
way into Christian literature.[4] The substance
of Gregory's use of the image is quite straight-
forward. Christ, he says, was the bringer of
light into a darkened world. Satan, on the
other hand, was the ruler of the darkness. So
when Christ entered the domain of Satan's self-
assumed jurisdiction, the latter became jealous
and attacked the "visible Adam," not realizing

---

1. Or. 43.64 (PG 36.581A), etc.
2. Or. 45.13 (PG 36.641A).
3. Or. 39.2, 12f (PG 36.336B, 349Af).
4. Greg. Nys., Cat. Or., 21; Augustine,
Serm. 130; Origen, Comm. in Mat., 16.8. A
possible use of this image may also be found
in Ignatius of Antioch, Eph. 19. See J. Rivière, "Le marché avec le démon chez les
Pères antérieurs à Saint Augustin," RevSR,
8 (1928), pp. 257-70.

that concealed behind what he could see was Christ's invisible and divine nature. Thus, at the very moment when Satan is sure of victory over the visible, he succumbs to defeat at the hands of the invisible. And Gregory adds that, it was only fitting that Satan, the σοφιστὴς τῆς κακίας, who had originally deceived the first Adam, should himself be deceived by the Second.[1]

However, this passing assent which Gregory gives to the defeat, through deception, of the Devil by the cross of Jesus Christ plays only a minor role in his thought. Much more important to him is his understanding of Christ as a ransom. Here, as with his treatment of the death of Christ as a sacrifice, Gregory makes constant use of the metaphor, but applies it in such a way that his own unique stamp is impressed upon it. Gregory is without doubt aware of the current theory that the death of Christ was a payment made by the Father to the Devil in order to redeem captive humanity from the latter's bondage. Gregory seemingly gives assent to this view when he speaks of Christ as a ransom (λύτρον) given for us as an "exchange," or when he claims that Christ redeems the world, and at a high price--the price of his own blood.[2] But this "ransom" vocabulary must not lead one into assuming that Gregory accepted the "ransom theory" as was then current, for he uses such words only as an instrument for probing even deeper into the mystery of salvation. To whom, he asks, was the ransom paid? And why? These are not idle questions or mere rhetorical devices for

---

1. Or. 39.13 (PG 36.349AB). Or. 40.10 (PG 36.369B) may possibly be another reference to the "deceit" of the Devil.
2. Or. 1.5 (PG 35.400A) and Or. 29.20 (PG 36.101A); see also Gregory's related discussion in Or. 30.20.

Gregory; they have to do, he says, with a matter of the highest importance, a _pragma_ and a _dogma_ that, although often neglected, demand close attention. In a famous and oft-quoted passage from _Oration_ 45, Gregory attempts to answer the very questions which he has raised:

> To whom was the blood offered and for
> what reason was it shed for us, that
> great and illustrious blood of God
> who is both High Priest and sacrifice?[1]

There would seem to be two viable alternatives: either the ransom was paid to the Devil or else it was paid to God. Gregory examines each of these alternatives in turn.

> We were prisoners of the Evil One, sold
> under sin and devoted to the pleasures
> of evil. If the ransom then belongs to
> none other than to the one who holds us
> captive, I ask, to whom was it given,
> and for what reason? If to the Evil
> One, what an outrage![2]

Thus Gregory joins the ranks of those few Greek Fathers who categorically deny that Christ's death was a ransom paid to the Devil.[3] He goes on to explain why it is that he refuses to accept

---

1. _Or._ 45.22 (PG 36.653A-C). Origen had asked the same question; see _Comm. in Mat._, 16.8.
2. _Or._ 45.22 (PG 36.643B).
3. Before Gregory, Pseudo-Adamantius (Methodius?) was equally determined to outlaw the possibility of having a ransom paid to the Devil; _De recta fide_, 1.27. John of Damascus was to repeat this as well as Gregory's views; _Exp. fidei orth._, 3.27. See Harnack, _DG_, 3, p. 291 and H. E. W. Turner, _The Patristic Doctrine of Redemption_ (London, 1952), pp. 58f and _passim._

any view which has the Evil One profit in any
way from Christ's sacrifice:

> If the robber gets a ransom, not only
> from God, but a ransom that also
> consists of God himself, and thus
> receives so immense a payment for his
> tyranny, it is a payment for the sake
> of which he might have done well to
> leave us alone.[1]

That is, how much more he might have received as
payment had he never deceived mankind in the first
place. But, as we shall see, "payment" is not a
category through which Gregory seeks to interpret
the death of Christ. Having rejected any ransom
being paid to Satan, Gregory then turns to the
second alternative and asks whether it be
acceptable:

> If then to the Father, let me ask
> first of all, How? For we were not
> under his power. And secondly, for
> what possible reason could the blood
> of his only-begotten Son have given
> pleasure to the Father, he who didn't
> even accept Isaac when offered by his
> father, but provided a ram in the place
> of the reasonable sacrifice. It is clear,
> then, that the Father neither asked for
> nor demanded the Son's sacrifice . . .[2]

Having said this much, however, Gregory cannot
rest satisfied with a mere rejection of the two

---

1. Or. 45.22 (PG 36.653B). Of the many
historians who have commented on Gregory's un-
willingness to have the Devil profit from
Christ's death, only Aulén (op. cit., p. 71), to
my knowledge, has seen cause to criticize
Gregory on this point.
2. Or. 45.22 (PG 653B).

alternatives. Christ's blood was paid neither
to the Evil One nor to the Father. But Christ's
blood <u>was</u> shed. So Gregory continues his last
phrase with the assertion that, although the
Father neither asked for nor demanded the price
of the Son's blood, he does nevertheless accept
(λαμβάνω) it. And the specific reason for
which God does accept it, according to Gregory,
is διὰ τὴν οἰκονομίαν.[1] In other words, God's
acceptance of the sacrifice is based upon the
fact that it is God who makes the sacrifice. The
divine <u>oikonomia</u>, as Gregory understands it,
cannot be limited to what the Son does for the
Father by way of reconciling mankind to the just
demands of God, or to the reconciliation of the
Father to a wayward creation. Rather, the divine
<u>oikonomia</u> has God, not only as its object, but
also as its subject. Gregory's insistence that
the Son is God stems from his assertion that God
himself is active in the economy of salvation.
To conceive of a transaction between the first
two Persons of the Godhead is absolutely
impossible given Gregory's triadological and
christological presuppositions. There can be no
thought in his writings, therefore, of a distant
Father who demands retribution from a temporarily

---

1. Ibid. This phrase is misleadingly
translated in <u>NPNF</u>, 7 (loc. cit.) as "on
account of the <u>incarnation</u>." Harnack (<u>DG</u> 3,p.
309) asserts that Gregory's statement that the
Father accepts the sacrifice of the Son διὰ τὴν
οἰκονομίαν is a manifest refusal to come to grips
with the problem since all Gregory means by that
phrase is "that the Scriptures might be fulfilled." F. Bonifas, also, accuses Gregory of
having no positive explanation of the non-
payment of ransom; <u>Histoire de l'église
chrétienne</u>, Vol. 2 (Paris, 1886), p. 202. Karl
Holl (op. cit., pp. 180ff) has, in my opinion,
both successfully countered these arguments and
interpreted Gregory more accurately.

absent Son for his (the Father's) wounded honor.
Gregory's God (Father, Son and Holy Spirit) is
a God who is himself the author of salvation, who
himself participates in mankind's fallen condition in order to redeem it. And this redemption
is through God's own suffering and death. The
Father, then, accepts the Son's sacrifice because
the Father is God; or, the Father accepts the
Son's sacrifice because the Son is God. There
can be neither request nor demand in such an
offering or in such an acceptance. The whole
motive behind the sacrifice is the salvation of
mankind, each Person of the Godhead playing a
distinct role, but all three roles undertaken
with a single, unitive purpose. Gregory explains,
therefore, what he means when he says that the
sacrifice is accepted by the Father διὰ τὴν
οἰκονομίαν by his assertion that:

> [I]t was necessary that man be sanctified
> by the humanity of God, so that, once
> the tyrant has been overpowered, the
> Father himself might set us free and
> lead us back to him through the mediation
> of the Son; and all this to the honor
> of the Father who was author of the plan.[1]

With this argument, Gregory has taken a current
and popular soteriological metaphor and employed
it in such a fashion that he has at the same time
avoided its possible "transactional" meaning and
centered its significance solely on the abiding
concern of God for his creation.

Christ, then, is, for Gregory, both a
"sacrifice" and a "ransom." As sacrifice, he is
both Priest and Victim; as ransom, he is God's
own payment of himself for mankind. By virtue
of the "power of the incarnation," the sanctification of mankind is achieved by God's active
participation in the very conditions of sin and
mortality from which we need to be saved.

---

1. Or. 45.22 (PG 36.653B).

But, we must point out, the "need" to be
saved, and the "need" for God to act in a particular way in order to effect salvation, are not
the same thing. Gregory is prone, we have seen,
to describe God's salvific economy as that
curative undertaking which was "necessary" for
our universal disease. Mankind, because of
the fall and the subsequent relative ineffecti-
veness of the Law and the Prophets, "needed" a
stronger remedy. It was necessary, further, if
the whole person was to be saved, for the incarnate
Son to be fully man and fully God. And the
sacrifice of Calvary was "necessary" to salvation. But all of these acts, for Gregory, stem,
not from a "divine" necessity, but from what we
might call an "economic" necessity, or, as
Stephan has so aptly phrased it, God's saving
acts arose not from an "absolute" necessity but
from a "relative" one.[1] Which is to say, the
means which God chose to save were, for mankind,
necessary means, but not for God. It was we who
"needed an incarnate God, a God put to death,"
if we were to live. But no logical or juridical
necessity was enjoined upon God so to act. Or,
as Florovsky has said, "The Cross was a necessity for human nature, not for divine justice."[2]
We cannot, therefore, fault the soteriological
arguments put forward by Gregory on account of
the "necessity" he claims for a particular kind
of incarnational union or for a specific variety
of salvific actions on the part of God. God,
says Gregory, could have chosen other methods;
he could have saved us, for instance, solely
through an act of the will (μόνῳ τῷ βούλεσθαι).[3]
The motive, then, behind Gregory's soteriology
is to proclaim, as he understands it, what God

---

1. Stephan, op. cit., p. 21.
2. Florovsky, Eastern Fathers, p. 120.
3. Ep. 101 (PG 37.188C). Cf. Wiles,
"Soteriological Arguments," pp. 321ff.

in fact has done "for us and for our salvation,"
and not to speculate either as to what God had
to do or to what God might have done.[1]

The high sense of drama with which Gregory
describes the passion and death of Christ as the
climax of the incarnation does not lead him,
characteristically, to view the cross as a
"violent" remedy for mankind's fallen condition.
The incarnation was indeed an "upsetting of the
laws of nature," and the transition from Law to
Gospel an "earthquake." Yet Gregory refuses to
see in the total economy of God anything other
than the gentle mercy and infinite patience of
a loving Creator unwilling to see his creation

---

1. As to the related questions of whether
or not the incarnation would have taken place
had there been no Fall, Gregory is silent; nor
is there any evidence that he gave this question
any thought. Yet it certainly would not be
inconsistent with his views to postulate an
incarnation as the independently planned means
of conducting mankind further on its pilgrimage
towards theōsis, although such an incarnation
would not have involved suffering and death.
See Florovsky's statement ("Lamb of God," p. 21):
"It seems to be more coherent to regard the
Incarnation as an organic consummation of the
primordial creative purpose of God as not to
make it essentially dependent on the Fall, i.e.,
upon the disruption of that purpose . . ." See
also Florovsky's discussion of this problem in
"Cur Deus Homo? The Motive of the Incarnation,"
Eucharisterion, Festival Volume on the 45th
Anniversary of Professor Hamilcar Alvisatos
(Athens, 1958). A note found in NPNF, 8 (p. 431,
n. λ) is also suggestive of this approach.

lost to him.[1] Even had God used violent measures
to effect salvation, suggests Gregory, they would
not have worked, since human pride was such that
too sudden or violent a remedy for our fallen
condition would only have increased our stubborn-
ness. Only a "gentle and kindly method of cure"
was likely to persuade us and turn us from
our godless idolatry. Mankind, continues Gregory,
is like a crooked sapling that will break in two
if forced too suddenly back into its proper
position.[2]

This image of fallen humanity as a "crooked
sapling" in need of a "non-violent remedy"
provides us with a new perspective on Gregory's
understanding of the place of the death of Christ
within the divine economy. It suggests, first
of all, that the remedy has been applied, and
primarily through the sacrifice of the incarnate
Son of God. But, in the second place, it
suggests that the cure is neither instantaneous
nor mechanical. We must examine each of these
points in turn.

(1) It cannot be denied that Gregory conceives of salvation as having been accomplished
primarily on Calvary. The cross, as we have
seen, is the climax of that action whereby God
reached down to raise a fallen creation. By the
divine assumption of human nature, human life,
and human death, the consequences of the Fall
have been undone. The cross is the symbol of
that victory over sin and death which has freed
us from poverty and bondage; sin and death have
been conquered, and the power of the Evil One
destroyed. When Gregory speaks of the resurrection, therefore, he does not describe it as the
means whereby the "defeat" on the cross is
miraculously turned into a "victory." The resurrection is not God's affirmation or recognition

---

1. Or. 45.12 (PG 36.637C-640B); see also
Or. 31.25 (PG 36.149BC) and Or. 38.2 (PG 36.313
B).
2. Or. 45.12 (PG 36.637C-640B).

of what the Son had done by way of suffering
obedience, nor a reward for it. Rather, the
resurrection followed the crucifixion because it
was God who had been crucified. The resurrection, therefore, is a continuation of the "power
of the incarnation." It is no surprise, then,
that, when we read Gregory's two Easter Sermons,
we find him speaking less of the resurrection
than of the cross. For him this is quite
natural. The resurrection is the anabasis which
marks the fulfillment of the katabasis. God
came down that we might go up. And mankind can
share in the resurrection of Christ by God's
total assumption, in him, of human nature, life,
and death; we share in the victory of what the
incarnate Son has accomplished. The old Adam
has been destroyed, and mankind rises with Christ
as a new creation.[2] The mystery of God become
man in Christ, proclaims Gregory in one of his
finest Orations, is ultimately expressed in his
crucifixion, which is our glorification; in
his death, which is our life; and in his
burial, which is our resurrection. And the
final meaning of this mystery is found in its
divine purpose; that we might become God.[3]

Thus, by means of the economy of the incarnation, salvation has been effected and the
remedy for mankind's universal disease applied.
Fallen humanity has been sanctified by the
humanity of God, i.e., by the "power of the
incarnation." The incarnate Son has entered
into the very depths of our fallen condition
and become a "leaven" to the whole "lump" of
mankind.[4] The world has been cleansed, the

---

1. Or. 1 (PG 35.396gg) and Or. 45 (PG
36.624ff).
2. Or. 40.45 (PG 36.421BC).
3. Or. 1.4 (PG 35.397BC), Or. 29.19 (PG
36.100A), Or. 38.13 (PG 36.325BC), and 1.2.10.
140-3 (PG 37.690), and elsewhere.
4. Or. 30.21 (PG 36.132B).

image has been restored, and the whole created order gathered unto God.[1]

(2) But, to refer to the image of the crooked sapling again, we must now ask, has the sapling become straight, even if the cure applied was gentle and not destructively violent? Gregory neither explicitly asks this question himself, nor does he provide us with a direct answer, but there is sufficient evidence within his own writings for us to formulate an answer for ourselves. The remedy has been applied, but the cure is still in process. Salvation can neither be instantaneous nor mechanical. In two separate but similar passages, Gregory reviews for his congregation the events of the incarnate life and death of Christ, and refers to the "titles" by which the Son is known. Walk through these titles, he says, and if you do it in a "godlike" manner, it is so that you might "become God" by rising from below, just as Christ for us became man by condescending from above.[2] Or, again, if we travel "faultlessly" through every stage and faculty of the life of Christ, we will rise with him, be glorified with him, and reign with him.[3]

In each of these passages a condition is overtly stated, a condition indicating that Gregory does not think of salvation as a fait accompli. Rather, we might say, salvation has been effected, but only in principio. The oikonomia of the incarnate Son is both the "beginning" of our salvation as well as the "principle" upon which it rests. Like the gentle remedy applied to the crooked sapling, salvation allows the tree to make full use of its own potential for growth. Were the pressure too sudden or too violent, the tree would snap.

---

1. Or. 38.13 (PG 36.325CD), Or. 45.2, 22 (PG 36.625A, 653BC).
2. Or. 30.21 (PG 35.133A).
3. Or. 38.18 (PG 36.332B-333A).

Which is to say, salvation has been achieved, but it must also be appropriated, and appropriated through the very potential for growth which is part of God's creative gift to mankind. The "gentle cure" therefore, is so that mankind might be persuaded. Rather than being mechanical or instantaneous, salvation, for Gregory, is a dynamic process (analogous to creation) which has been set in motion.

Such a view is thoroughly in harmony with Gregory's anthropology and christology. His understanding of human nature, as we have already shown, centers less on a static definition of our constituent parts than it does on an appreciation of the dynamic purposes for which we were created, i.e., our vocation of theōsis as the continuing growth towards the understanding of God and participation in the divine life. And Gregory's understanding of Christ, as has also been pointed out, is derived less from a static delineation of how two "natures" can appear in one "person" than from a conviction as to the dynamic purpose of the incarnation, seen not only in the assumption of human nature, but also of human life and death.

The image of the "sapling," therefore, is very germane to Gregory's view of salvation. It includes the concept which underlies the economy of creation, namely, that of growth; it also includes the concept which underlies the economy of the incarnation, namely, that of patient, gentle condescension to human existence. Accordingly, all of mankind has been saved. Yet we must say that this salvation is more of a beginning than an end. As saved, we remain creatures with a vocation. As saved, we still have free will, which means that our salvation

---

1. Persuasion, not violence, is thus also the appropriate means whereby the pastor leads his flock; Or. 2.15 (PG 35.424C). See also Irenaeus, Adv. haer., 5.1.1 and Spidlik, op. cit., p. 72.

can never be a matter of coercion. The "gentle
cure" is that we might be persuaded, not up-
rooted or broken in two. In effect, we must
choose the salvation that has already been
accomplished for us. As the Father "received"
the sacrificial and redeeming blood of his Son,
so too must the Christian "receive" the benefits
of that divine gift.

Mankind, by virtue of the economy of the
incarnation, has the restored and renewed
vocation of moving once more on its Godward
pilgrimage, sure again of both its direction and
speed. We live now in a new and "changed" world,
a change represented by the fact that, although
we are still surrounded by the outward manifestations of fallen creation, these are no longer
an ultimate barrier to our progress. The
theōsis which was our created destiny has become
now our re-created destiny.

The resurrection and ascension of Jesus
Christ, says Gregory, terminate that series of
salvific events by which God wrought our salvation in Christ Jesus. The "economy of the Body
of Christ" has come to an end.[1] The birth,
baptism, betrayal, death, burial, resurrection
and ascension are now all past.[2] What is to
come, however, Gregory claims to be even "more
glorious," namely, the fulfillment of both
Christ's "promise" and our "hope."[3] The
"economy of the Body of Christ" has been completed; now the "economy of the Spirit is beginning."[4]

---

1. Or. 41.5 (PG 36.536B).
2. Or. 38.2 (PG 36.313BC) and Or. 40.45
(PG 36.424).
3. Or. 41.5 (PG 36.436BC).
4. Ibid.

CHAPTER VI -- THE ECONOMY OF THE HOLY SPIRIT

One of the more memorable formulas by which Gregory attempts to describe his concept of the Trinity is: φῶς, καὶ φῶς, καὶ φῶς· ἀλλ'ἐν φῶς, εἷς θεός.[1] As he had fought against the Arians in order to proclaim the full divinity of the Son, so too he contends against the Pneumatomachians, or "Spirit-fighters," in order to assert the full deity of the third Person of the Trinity. In each case, he argues from an identical premise, namely, that all three hypostaseis of the Godhead share in one ousia, and that the "relation" between them is one, not of graduated subordination, but of individuated "properties." The Father, as we have seen, is designated γεννήτωρ or ἄναρχος, and the Son γέννημα or γεννητός. Gregory has a similar designation for the Holy Spirit: πρόβλημα or ἐκπορευτός.[2] This "procession" of the Spirit, however, like the "generation" of the Son, is beyond the categories of time, causality, or materiality. Gregory pokes fun at those who think in such categories when referring to the Persons of the Godhead, accusing them of being forced into the ridiculous position of asserting a "Father God," a "Son," and a "Grandson God."[3] Yet, for all of Gregory's varied attempts to explain to his own, as well as to his opponents', satisfaction how it is that the Spirit can "proceed" from the Father, he is forced finally, as he was when explaining the

---

1. Or. 31.3 (PG 36.136C). The three "lights" analogy was, as we have already seen, used previously to describe God, angels, and humankind.

2. Or. 29.2 (PG 36.76B), Or. 31.9 (PG 36.141C-144A), etc. See also Or. 29.12 (PG 36.348B). Cf. Basil Caes., De Spiritu sancto, 1-5 (PG 32.68-81), and P. Galtier, Le Saint Esprit en nous d'après les pères grecs (Rome, 1946), p. 179.

3. Or. 31.10 (PG 36.144A).

"generation" of the Son, to admit that such things are
incomprehensible mysteries. It is unwise, he says, to
try to understand the "procession of the Spirit," unwise, that is, to delve too inquisitively into the
"mystery of God."[1] Nevertheless, in spite of the ac-
knowledged limits of reason and of language, Gregory
presses his arguments with unflagging zeal. We worship,
he proclaims, "God the Father, God the Son, and--don't
let this upset you--God the Holy Spirit."[2] And, with
what must have appeared to him as unassailable logic,
he continues: "Is the Spirit God? Certainly. Is the
Spirit therefore homoousion? If he is God, he must
be!"[3]

Gregory is quite self-conscious about breaking new
ground here, aware that he is crossing terminological
barriers seldom crossed before. As early as 372 he
claims that it is high time to remove the candle from
under the bushel and proclaim clearly, without resort-
ing to safe but devious "metaphors" or "rough sketches,"
the fullness of the Godhead, including the declaration
that the Spirit is God.[4] A decade later, in one of his
letters to Cledonius, Gregory refers to the Symbol of
Nicaea as the standard of orthodoxy, especially in respect to its successful destruction of the "Arian heresy." But, he adds, the Fathers at Nicaea spoke "incom-
pletely" of the Spirit, since all they said was, "And
[we believe] in the Holy Spirit." Accordingly, Gregory
tells Cledonius that he feels it to be his vocation to
make up for the deficiency of the Nicene Symbol and to
"confess that the Spirit also is God."[5] In another context, Gregory looks back to the Synod of Alexandria in
362 and congratulates Athanasius, its convener, for
having been the first--or at least among the first--to
venture, in public and in writing, an explicit avowal
of the full deity of the Holy Spirit. Gregory expresses

---

1. Or. 31.10 (PG 36.144A).
2. Or. 33.16 (PG 36.236A).
3. Or. 31.10 (PG 36.144A).
4. Or. 12.6 (PG 36.849BC).
5. Ep. 102 (PG 37.193C).

122

his regrets, however, that so few people at that time or since accepted Athanasius' views.[1]

One of the reasons that Gregory knew he was breaking new ground is that his opponents were constantly pressing him to explain the "novelty" of his doctrine of the full deity of the Spirit. Well aware that "novelty" was a term of opprobrium used to suggest "heresy," Gregory does, in fact, admit that his doctrine is new, but at the same time will argue for its doctrinal authenticity.[2] In his explanation of why this doctrine had not been accepted explicitly by the church earlier, Gregory has recourse to two theories.

(1) The first reason he gives we might call the "diplomatic" approach. He brings this argument forward when attempting to explain why his friend Basil, when Bishop of Caesarea, had failed to state clearly that the Spirit is God.[3] Gregory claims that Basil did in fact assent to the "consubstantiality" of the Spirit, but, for reasons of tact, avoided making such a statement publicly. Basil did, however, adds Gregory, confess in private to him that the Spirit is homoousion with the Father and the Son. The reason that Basil avoided any open reference to the full deity of the Spirit is that he had to resort to the device of theological tact so as not to embarrass his supporters and --more important--not to give his enemies any cause to misunderstand him. Since the "heretics" were in the majority, it would not be wise to provide them with too ready an excuse, given the theologically unsettled climate in Cappadocia, to call him a "heretic." Yet, a careful examination of Basil's writings, Gregory continues, will reveal that he did believe the Spirit to be God, although he never said as much in so many words. Thus Gregory exonerates his friend, excusing his terminological hesitation on the grounds of an "economy

---

1. Or. 21.33-4 (PG 35.1121C-1124B); see Athanasius, Tomus ad Antiochenos, 3.
2. See H. E. W. Turner, The Pattern of Christian Truth (London, 1954), pp. 3-35.
3. Or. 43.68 (PG 36.588AB).

of tactful diplomacy." Implicit in Gregory's arguments, however, is the suggestion that the "novelty" of
a doctrine need not derive solely from its not having been
explicitly articulated before (an argument that will
serve to support many "new" doctrines in the centuries
to come!).[1]

(2) But more important than his attempt to defend
Basil's theological reluctance is Gregory's recourse
to what we will call "scriptural economy" as the reason
for the "lateness" of the doctrine of the Spirit. His
opponents had asked Gregory, "Whence have you brought
us this alien and unscriptural God?"[2] Gregory replies
that, although Scripture is silent as to the theotēs
of the Spirit, this certainly does not mean that the
Spirit is a strange or alien God. It would be to limit
ourselves, he continues, to the letter of the Scriptures. After all, the Bible speaks as of God as a
body, when we know perfectly well that he has not; the
Bible speaks of a God who sleeps, walks around, gets
angry, etc., but we know that such language is merely
an attempt to describe the indescribable through recourse to human analogy.[3] In like manner, we must not
be too disturbed by what the Bible does not say, since
it is evident that throughout Scripture there is a
steady unfolding of truth, an oikonomia of gradual
revelation:

> The Old Testament openly proclaimed the
> Father, but proclaimed the Son only
> dimly; the New Testament manifested the
> Son, but only hinted at the deity of the
> Spirit; and now the Spirit lives in our
> midst, providing us with a clearer demon-
> stration of himself. For it was not safe

---

1. Ibid. On the relation between Basil and Gregory
on the doctrine of the Holy Spirit, see H. Dörries,
De Spiritu Sancto (Göttingen, 1956), pp. 26-8, and
B. Pruche in SC, 17 (bis), pp. 82ff.
2. Or. 31.1, 21 (PG 36.133B, 156C).
3. Ibid., 1. 22 (PG 36.133B, 157AB).

> for the Son to be proclaimed openly un-
> til the deity of the Father was confessed,
> nor for the deity of the Holy Spirit to
> be added as a burden until that of the Son
> was accepted.[1]

It was for this reason, Gregory continues, that Christ himself refrained from revealing everything to his disciples at the outset. Many truths he kept from them, either because they were not sufficiently advanced to understand them, or because they might easily have been alienated from Christ had he told them too much. But one thing Christ did tell his disciples, that he would send them the Spirit. It was to be by the indwelling of this same Spirit that they would be led into all truth. And, of the many things that the Spirit would teach them, certainly the truth concerning his as yet unacknowledged deity would be one.[2]

Gregory appears to be the first patristic author to use this theory of "progressive revelation" to explain the "novelty" of a doctrine, a doctrine which in this case asserts the full deity of the Spirit.[3] On the surface he might be accused of evading the issues or of refusing to explain details, as indeed he has been. One author, for instance, criticizes him on just this point, saying that Gregory is too "cautious," although such caution "harmonizes well with the theological nervousness which St. Gregory displays in his dealings with the Pneumatomachi."[4] Gregory does, indeed, as we have noticed on several occasions, admit his inability to articulate theological formulas which will satisfy everyone, but he cannot be accused of evasion or caution. In fact, as we shall see, in his doctrine of the

---

1. Ibid., 26 (PG 36.161C).
2. Ibid., 27 (PG 36.164BC).
3. See Kelly, Early Christian Doctrines, p. 261, and R. P. C. Hanson, "Basil's Doctrine of Tradition in Relation to the Holy Spirit," VC, 22, No. 4 (Dec., 1968), pp. 241-55.
4. So H. E. W. Turner, op. cit., pp. 266-7.

Holy Spirit, there is considerably more boldness of conviction and vigor of expression than such criticisms
are willing to admit.

Whether it be his recourse to an "economy of diplomacy" or an "economy of revelation," Gregory uses such
arguments only to still the noisome pestilence of his
opponents. They are merely negative expressions of his
own positive doctrine. The term homoousion, when applied
to the Spirit, Gregory knows to be a "stumbling block"
and "stone of offence" to those who quibble over words,
syllables, or even letters (i.e., iotas).[1] For this
reason, Gregory seeks constantly to phrase and re-
phrase, the more accurately to persuade his opponents
of what he believes to be the truth concerning the
Spirit. The Spirit, he says, always has been, is, and
always will be; he is without beginning or cause.[2] The
Spirit shares in the one ousia of the Godhead, but the
Godhead is not thereby divided; rather, there are divi-
sions "in relation to the ousia of the Godhead."[3] Yet,
within the Godhead, and common to each of the hypos-
tases, there is an "identity of essence and power."[4]

These assertions, as is most apparent, are identical to those by which Gregory sought to proclaim the
full deity of the Son, although in this case his theological opponents are of a different sort, having no
questions, as did the Arians, about the consubstantiality of the Son. But the real testing ground of Gregory's doctrine of the Holy Spirit is not to be found
in his repetition of trinitarian formulas, any more
than it is in his appeals to the progressive nature
of revelation or the current need for theological
tact. Nor does his doctrine rest primarily upon the
fact of the Spirit's own testimony concerning himself.
All these arguments are used, but the ultimate base
for Gregory's view is to be discovered by direct

---

1. Or. 41.7 (PG 36.437B-440A).
2. Ibid., 9 (PG 36.441A).
3. Ibid.
4. Or. 31.16 (PG 36.152B); see also Or. 2.39 (PG
35.448A).

reference to his understanding of the economy of salvation. As his christological arguments stemmed primarily from his concern that the "whole man" be saved, so too his pneumatology is grounded upon and arises out of specifically soteriological convictions.

Gregory's understanding of salvation, as we have seen, has its initial roots in his doctrine of creation. God created the world with the specific purpose of having mankind fulfill progressively its divinely ordained destiny of theōsis. If the Spirit, then, is God, he must have participated in the economy of creation. And so he did, asserts Gregory. Quoting a passage from Job, he makes his point quite clear: "It is the divine spirit (πνεῦμα) that made me, and the breath (πνοή) of the Almighty that has taught me."[1] And from the Psalmist:

> By the Word (λόγος) of the Lord were the
>   heavens made,
> And by the breath (πνεῦμα) of his mouth,
>   all their power.[2]

God conceived the world, says Gregory elsewhere, and this conception was "fulfilled" by his Word and "perfected" by his Spirit.[3] Here again we see Gregory's constant conviction as to the union of the Godhead, with the unity of purpose shared equally by each of the three Persons within the Godhead.

And the Spirit, because he is God, shares not only in creation, but also in the economy of the incarnation.[4] Making innumerable references to Gospel

---

1. Or. 41.14 (PG 36.448B); Job 33.4.
2. Ibid.; Ps. (LXX) 32.6.
3. Or. 38.9 (PG 36.320C). In this instance Gregory is speaking of the "first" (angelic) creation, but what he says of the creative activity of the Spirit can be applied to all three stages of the creative purpose.
4. Nor was the Spirit inactive between the time of creation and the time of the incarnation; the

passages, Gregory portrays the constant activity of the
Spirit during the life of the incarnate Son: the Spirit
was the forerunner of Christ's birth, the witness to
his baptism, his guide and succor during the temptation,
the co-worker of his miracles.[1] The Spirit continually
indwelt the Son, but not, Gregory warns, as an "energizing power," but as one accompanying his equal.[2]

From creation to resurrection, then, the eternal
Spirit shares in the economy of salvation, and precisely because he is God. Or, as Gregory puts it, the Spirit "shares with the Son both the work of creation and
of resurrection."[3] As the Son is ὁ τεχνίτης λόγος, so
the Spirit is πνεῦμα τὸ ποιῆσαν.[4]

Thus, since the author of the economy of salvation
is God, and since the Spirit is God, Gregory will
passionately deny that the Spirit is a "new" or "alien"
God. But, at the same time, he conceives of the work of
the Spirit as belonging more to the present than to the
past. In the unfolding oikonomia of God's providential
love for his creation the Spirit has his particular--
though not exclusive--role to play after the "economy

---

patriarchs and prophets lived through the "power of the
Spirit." Or. 41.11, 14 (PG 36.444B, 448A-449A).

1. Or. 31.29 (PG 36.165AB). It is not surprising
that Gregory here fails to mention any specific role
of the Spirit in the conception of Christ since the
phrase "conceived by the Holy Spirit" was not yet a
part of the Eastern credal tradition. Gregory's version
of the Spirit's role in this case was that, prior to
the conception of Jesus, Mary was "purified by the Holy
Spirit" (no need, therefore, for a prior "immaculate
conception"), although the Spirit was not himself the
agent of conception. See Or. 38.13 (PG 36.325B) and
1.1.9.67-9 (PG 37.462).

2. Or. 41.11 (PG 36.444B). The view, common among
the Gnostics, that the Spirit indwelt Christ as an
energizing dynamis seems to have had its adherents in
Gregory's day as well.

3. Ibid., 14 (PG 36.448A).

4. Or. 31.29 (PG 36.165C).

of the body of Christ" has been complete. Parallel to
Gregory's concept of the economy of revelation, in
which the deity of the Spirit is made known only after
the resurrection and ascension of Christ, is his concept of the special work of the Spirit in the re-created
world for which God had given his blood as a sacrifice.
This special role is to perfect, for mankind, the work
of redemption wrought by God in Christ. In one passage
Gregory refers to the Trinity as the "three greatest"
and assigns to each of the three Persons a specific
role: to the Father, αἴτιος, to the Son, δημιουργός,
and to the Spirit, τελειοποιός.[1] Therefore, when Gregory says that it is the Spirit himself who witnesses
to his own deity, it is because what the Spirit does,
i.e., perfecting, can be achieved by none other than
God. The witness of the Spirit is made manifest through
his perfecting of what has already been fully accomplished, but only potentially made available, through
the economy of the incarnation. This is because, as
Gregory says, the Spirit is God in the world, God con-
taining all things and filling all things.[2]

In seeking to determine the dimensions of Gregory's
doctrine of the Spirit, it might be helpful to suggest
the following formulation. If the incarnate Son of God
is the agent of redemption for mankind in general, the
Spirit is the agent of providing for us, individually,
the means whereby we can appropriate that redemption.
What Christ has accomplished universally, the Spirit
perfects particularly.[3] Gregory does not say this himself, in so many words, but that it is a valid

---

1. Or. 34.8 (PG 36.249A).
2. Or. 31.29 (PG 36.165C).
3. Christ, for Gregory, assumed not an individual
man but human nature; the Spirit, on the other hand,
although universally present, is individually operative. V. Lossky has suggested the following formulation in this concept: the work of the Son is for human
"nature"; the work of the Spirit is for the human
"person." "Redemption and Deification," Sob, Ser. 3,
No. 2 (1947), p. 55.

interpretation of his thought can be shown through a
more detailed examination of the vocabulary by which
he describes the work of the Spirit.

In his first Easter Oration, Gregory says, "May he
that rose today from the dead also recreate me (κἀμὲ
καινοποιήσῃ) by the Spirit."[1] That is, the new creation
effected by the work of Christ, in his assumption of
our common nature, life and death, is communicated
individually--"to me"--by the Spirit. Gregory uses many
words to define the nature of the re-creative activity
of the Spirit, all of them drawn from the New Testament: the Spirit is perfecter, fulfiller, and sancti-
fier.[2] The Spirit's deity rests ultimately, for Gregory, on these functions, a deity that is not "by
adoption" but "by nature," a deity not all his own but
of the essence of the Godhead. For what the Spirit does
is precisely what God does.[3] But more than all this,
it is the work of the Spirit to be the individual person's source of direction along the path of theōsis.
It is for this reason that V. Lossky, in reflecting
upon the patristic tradition regarding deification,
has said: ". . . the idea of our ultimate deification
cannot be expressed on a christological basis alone,
but demands a pneumatological development of doctrine."[4] This is eminently true of Gregory. He begins
his poem, De Spiritu sancto, for instance, with the
following words:

> Why hesitatest thou, my soul? Sing also
> Thy praises of the Spirit, but destroy it not
> With fables which beyond its nature go.
> Let us tremble before the great Spirit,
> Like unto God he is, and God by him have I known.
> Yet, more than this, God he is,
> And me he deifies here below.[5]

---

1. Or. 1.2 (PG 35.396C-397A).
2. Or. 41.9 (PG 36.441B).
3. Or. 31.29 (PG 36.165C).
4. Lossky, op. cit., p. 51.
5. 1.1.2.1-4 (PG 37.408).

130

In the Fifth Theologian Oration, Gregory's argument is less poetic but considerably more direct:

> If the Spirit is of the same order or
> creation as myself, how can he deify
> me or join me to the Godhead? . . .
> If he is a creature . . . how are we
> perfected in him?[1]

And Gregory's oratory is even more persistent when he defies those who would belittle the Spirit:

> If the Holy Spirit is not God, let him
> first be deified, and then let him deify
> me his equal![2]

In such language we see Gregory making considerably more use of the "first person singular" than when discussing the economy of the incarnation. This lends weight to the statement that, whereas Christ saves mankind, the Spirit perfects that salvation for the individual. That the Spirit is both God and deifier is an essential element, then, not only of Gregory's doctrine of the Trinity, but of his understanding of the economy of salvation. Yet it is in that most "individual" and "personal" of Christian rites, baptism, where Gregory sees the chief work of the Spirit as taking place. In baptism, the primary locus of the Spirit's deifying action, the "universal salvation" wrought by Christ becomes the "particular salvation" of the individual person.

More than being only a rite of initiation into the Christian church, baptism is the means by which a person participates in Christ's victory over sin, death, and the Evil One. Accordingly, the baptizand is initiated less into the church, per se, than into the "new creation." The outward manifestations of the old creation are still very much in evidence, but,

---

1. Or. 31.4, 6 (PG 36.137B, 140B).
2. Or. 34.12 (PG 36.252C).

after baptism, these have no more power over the Christian. Baptism, generally referred to by Gregory, as by most Eastern Fathers, as an "illumination," provides inestimable benefits. Gregory enumerates them as follows:

A help for our weakness,
a putting off of the flesh,
a following of the Spirit,
communion with the Logos,
an emendment of the creature,
the wiping away of sin,
the possession of light,
the overcoming of darkness,
a vehicle which leads towards God,
a travelling with Christ,
a support for one's faith,
perfection of the mind,
a key to the Kingdom of Heaven,
an exchange for life,
removal of one's chains,
and the transformation of man's
    synthetic nature.[1]

One has the feeling that Gregory could continue this "catalogue" of the benefits of baptism almost indefinitely, so insistent is he upon convincing his congregation of its importance. Many other terms he uses as well in order to underline the salvific work of the Spirit in baptism: it is a "new birth" and a "re-creation"; it is the "formation" and "perfection" of us κατὰ Χριστόν .[2] In even more dramatic terms, baptism is the "re-forging" of a person, but without fire, "re-building" or "putting together" without having to be broken apart.[3] By submitting to the cleansing

---

1. Or. 40.3 (PG 36.361B).
2. Or. 39.2 (PG 36.336B), Or. 18.13 (PG 35.1001A). See also 1.1.3.44-5 (PG 37.411). Cf. Origen, De princ. 3.5.6-7 and Greg. Nys., Orat. cat. 26.
3. Or. 40.8 (PG 36.368B). Gregory of Nyssa,

waters, something "new" is added; we are no longer
our "old" selves. Or, as Gregory puts it, in line
with his concept of the divine vocation of mankind,
we are made "godlike."[1]

These many terms by which Gregory attempts to explain the "mystery" of baptism are but variations on
a single theme, namely, that of the "deifying" operation of the Holy Spirit who is God. Baptism "into the
Father," says Gregory, is Jewish; baptism into the
"Father and Son" is better; but baptism into the
"Father, Son, and Holy Spirit . . . whose common name
is God" is best of all.[2] Accordingly, as Gregory is
convinced of the deity of the Spirit because only God
can "deify," so he sees in baptism the primary individual means of appropriating the "deifying" work of
Christ for mankind: "If the Spirit is not worshipped as
God, how can he deify me through baptism?"[3] Or, again,
"If I worshipped a creature, or was baptized into a
creature, I would not be deified." And, " Baptism in
the Spirit is the perfect baptism. How then is the
Spirit not God--if I may be a little presumptuous--if
it is by him that you are made God?"[4]

It becomes increasingly clear, as we study Gregory's doctrines of the Holy Spirit and of baptism,
that there is here a constant building on ground that
we have already covered. Gregory's understanding of
the divine economy and of the dynamics of salvation
inform him every step of the way, from his concept of
the theological vocation through the benevolent act
of creation and the various stages whereby God has
sought to bring fallen mankind back to the original

---

however, will say (Or. cat., 8) that the external,
sentient part of man must be broken, just as a potter
breaks a clay mold before its internal shape can be
restored.

1. Or. 40.8 (PG 36.368B).
2. Or. 33.17 (PG 36.236C).
3. Or. 31.8 (PG 36.165A).
4. Or. 39.17 (PG 36.353C-356A), Or. 40.42 (PG
36.420A).

progressive purposes for which it was created, even to the "present," when each individual has the opportunity, under the economy of the Holy Spirit, to claim for him or herself the redemption wrought for all by God in Christ. The controlling principle throughout is soteriological, a principle that finds its most consistent expressing in Gregory's use of the term theōsis. We were originally created by God with the divinely ordained destiny of theōsis. When we strayed from this original purpose, God assumed human nature, condescended to the level of human life, and sacrificed himself on the cross, all so as to restore to us the potential for fulfilling the original destiny of theōsis, a destiny of which we had been deprived by the deception of the Evil One, by sin, and by the resulting mortality. And, finally, God provided mankind with the means whereby what had been effected corporately could be appropriated individually, the chief of which is the "mystery" of baptism, the arena of the activity of the Holy Spirit.

Gregory's stress on the deificatory role of the Spirit in baptism is equalled only by the zeal with which he commends baptism to his congregation. He refers often to what seems to have been the fairly common practice of postponing baptism, but avoids (we notice) any mention of the postponement of his own baptism.[1] He is nevertheless adamant in his condemnation of such practice, and quick to call in support of his views the Johannine dictum that "no one is able to see or receive the Kingdom who has not been reborn from above by the Spirit."[2] In almost studied juxtaposition with his exaltation of the benefits of

---

1. K. Aland, among others, has been quick to point out the discrepancy between Gregory's insistence upon the dangers of putting off baptism and his own postponed baptism; Did the Early Church Baptize Infants? (London, 1963), p. 41, n. 4. Cf. J. Jeremias, Infant Baptism in the First Four Centuries (London, 1960), p. 88.

2. Or. 41.14 (PG 36.448C), Jn. 3:3, 5.

baptism, Gregory spells out in unmistakable detail the
dangers involved in its being put off. The unbaptized
person is easy prey for the Devil who will tempt the
unsuspecting victim by saying: "Give me the present,
and give God the future; give me your youth, and give
God your old age; give me your desire for pleasures,
and give God the time when you are no longer able to
enjoy them."[1] By putting off baptism, says Gregory,
you are putting off your most priceless treasure,
Christ; by putting off baptism, you are plotting against
your own salvation.[2] Gregory has heard all the arguments used to support those who wished to delay baptism,
and he has ready answers for each of them. The laborers
who were hired at the last hour still received a full
day's wage; yes, but they were not called until the
last hour, whereas you are called now. God is surely
merciful enough to honor the "intention" of baptism as
well as the "fact" of baptism; yes, but you do not hang
someone just because he "intended" to commit murder,
any more than God will reward one for just wanting to
be baptized. There is always the danger of falling
again into sin; yes, but only in baptism are the
weapons provided by which one can protect oneself from
such a danger.[3]

Gregory's insistence on the present need for baptism includes the need for children to be baptized.
Infants, however, probably should not be baptized,
except in extremis. Otherwise, children should wait
until they are at least three years of age, or until a
time when they are able to grasp at least the rudi-
mentary meaning of baptism and make some response for
themselves.[4]

---

1. Or. 40.14 (PG 36.376C).
2. Ibid., 16, 18 (PG 36.377C, 381CD).
3. Ibid., 16-23 (PG 36.377C-389C).
4. Ibid., 28 (PG 36.400AB). Gregory goes on to say
that those infants who die unbaptized will not be
punished, since they have not sinned, but neither
will they be glorified, since they have not received
the "seal." It has been suggested that Gregory is

Gregory is also careful to point out that there is the added danger of being baptized into the wrong faith, i.e., into a faith which fails to recognize the full deity of all three persons of the Trinity. Being baptized into a faith that is doctrinally wanting may, he warns his congregation, result not in a "baptism" but in a "drowning" (καταβαπτιστής)![1] But if Gregory recommends caution as to the faith into which one is baptized, he puts no reservations on the choice of persons by whom one is baptized. "Do not ask," he advises, "for the credentials of the administrant," or think that baptism at the hands of a bishop is more efficacious than one performed by a humble priest. Anyone can baptize, but the grace of baptism is always the same, since the regenerative power of baptism is the work of the Holy Spirit, not of the administrant. More pertinent than a misguided pride in the baptizer is the personal humility of the baptized, the same humility whereby Christ, into whom we are baptized, took upon himself the form of a servant and was himself baptized, though, being God, he had no need of it.[2]

---

here giving a primitive outline of the later more fully developed concept of limbo; see L. Lyonnet, "Le péché originel en Rom 5, 12," Bib, 41 (1960), pp. 342ff. Cf. N. P. Williams, op. cit., pp. 288-91. Gregory also points to a difference between adult and infant baptism; in the case of infants or children, baptism confers a "seal," while in the case of adults, who presumably have sinned, added to the "seal" are baptismal "grace" and "restoration." Or. 40.7 (PG 36.365C); cf. 1.1.9.91-2 (PG 37.464).
    1. Or. 40.44 (PG 36.421C).
    2. Or. 40.26-7 (PG 36.396A-396A). When speaking of the credentials of the administrant, Gregory seems to have Novatus in mind, although he does not mention him by name in this passage; but see Or. 33.16 (PG 36.233C), Or. 39.19 (PG 36.357BC), and Or. 40.18-19 (PG 36.381B-384C). Be it noted that Gregory nowhere makes a distinction between lay and clerical baptism, but from his silence no specific conclusions can be drawn.

Salvation, because it is a present necessity, demands that baptism be undertaken now, and not later; that it be into the orthodox (i.e., trinitarian), not heretical, faith. Yet, for all of Gregory's insistence on these points, it would be a mistake to conclude that he thereby automatically excludes the possibility of salvation for those who are not baptized.[1] Preaching to a congregation that includes a group of baptizands awaiting their "illumination," and aware of the presence of the same congregation of others whom he had as yet been unable to lead to the "holy font," Gregory quite naturally presses his arguments for baptism with all the rhetorical vigor at his command. To this latter group he says, "As long as you are catechumens you are only on the outer threshold of religion. You must be inside; you must come through the vestibule, observe the holy rites, peer into the Holy of Holies, and be with the Trinity."[2] Gregory thus speaks directly to the need for baptism if one is to be saved. Yet he also speaks indirectly to the various possibilities of non-sacramental baptism. Some instances of this can be discovered by reference to Gregory's own writings.

In one passage, for instance, Gregory says that there are _five_ kinds of baptism: there is (a) the "figurative" baptism of Moses in the water, (b) the "preparatory" baptism of John which was "unto repentance," (c) the "perfect" baptism of Christ in the Spirit, (d) the glorious baptism of martyrdom and blood, which Christ also underwent, and (e) finally

---

1. J. Korbacher has made just this mistake; although concerned only with "baptism by desire" (which Gregory specifically denies), he interprets Gregory's "rigoristic" statements at face value, and avoids the implications of his "laxist" statements by appealing to the context in which they appear, concluding categorically that the unbaptized are, for Gregory, _ipso facto_ damned: "Eine Heilsmöglichkeit für sie kennt Gregor nicht." _Ausserhalb der Kirche kein Heil?_ (München, 1963), pp. 208-12.

2. _Or_. 40.16 (_PG_ 36.380B).

there is the "penitential" baptism of tears. In this
last category Gregory includes the repentance of Menas-
seh, the humility of the Ninevites, the "justification"
of the tax collector, as well as the Canaanite woman
who begged crumbs from her master's table.[1] In another
context he refers again to this baptism of penitence,
comparing the "painless" baptism of the Spirit to the
"painful" baptism of tears: "How many tears must we
shed before they serve as a substitute for the waters
of baptism?"[2] Again, Gregory devotes an entire Oration
to the memory of the pre-Christian Maccabean martyrs,
portraying them as the prototype of later Christian
martyrs. Their martyrdom, he claims, was a true sacrifice and libation, a fulfillment and perfection, a
model for Christians to imitate. And the great mystery
of what they were able to do is that, apart from faith
in Christ, they would not have achieved their goal.
The incarnation, indeed, took place after their time,
but the Logos was known earlier to those who were pure
in heart.[3] Gregory also refers constantly to the prophets and patriarchs of the Old Testament, describing
them in terms which have a definite salvific ring to
them: "blessed" Hosea, the "divine" Micah, the "sanctified" Jeremiah, etc. There can be no doubt that Gregory included such pre-Christians within the economy of
salvation, for they themselves, as we have already seen,
played a direct instrumental role in that economy.[4]

---

1. Or. 39.17 (PG 353C-356A). Gregory also claims
that Christ's real baptism was his passion and death,
thus countering the argument that his baptism by water
at the age of thirty was a precedent for postponing
the rite; Or. 40.29 (PG 36.400C-401A).
    2. Or. 40.9 (PG 36.369A).
    3. Or. 15.2 (PG 35.913AB). See D. F. Winslow, "The
Maccabean Martyrs: Early Christian Attitudes," Jud,
23, No. 1 (Winter, 1974), pp. 78-86; also M. Schatkin,
"The Maccabean Martyrs," VC, 28, No. 2 (June, 1974),
pp. 97-113.
    4. See Gregory's panegyric on the OT prophets in
Or. 2.57-67 (PG 35.468B-477A).

It cannot be claimed, therefore, that Gregory's concept of baptism is so rigid as to exclude pre-Christians from its ultimate benefits, either the worthies of the Old Testament, or those persons whom he describes from the New. His understanding of the work of the pre-incarnate Logos, as well as his view of the eternal role of the Holy Spirit, precludes his being so narrowly exclusivistic. He states, for instance, in his encomium on Athanasius, that when that great Alexandrian died, he was gathered to God along with the prophets and patriarchs, and all those who had "contended for the truth."[1] Christian baptism in Christ by the Spirit, therefore, may be the "perfect" baptism, but it is certainly not the only baptism.

This is equally true of those living in the Christian era. He speaks, for instance, of his sister Gorgonia who, like him, was not baptized until she had reached maturity. But, says Gregory (and can this be a disguised excuse for his own postponed baptism?), the purity and perfection of her life were so great that, even though she did finally receive the "regeneration of the Holy Spirit," the benefits of that sacrament were already assured her by virtue of her former life.[3] Gregory uses similar words of his father. When he was

---

1. Or. 21.37 (PG 35.1128AB). Gregory gives no evidence that he thought those outside the OT tradition (e.g., Socrates, Plato, etc.) to be without the possibility of salvation. He does, however, say that the Lord's descent into Hell was so that all might be received, at least all who made a response of faith. Or. 45.24 (PG 36.657AB).

2. An admission of the divinity of the Spirit is therefore not a necessary part of extra-sacramental baptism, especially in the case of pre-Christian "saints." Yet the Spirit is operative, as we have seen, in all baptisms. See Or. 31.29 (PG 36.163A). See also L. Capéran, Le problème du salut des infidèles: essai historique (Paris, 1912), pp. 179 f, n. 3.

3. Or. 8.20 (PG 35.992BC).

baptized, claims his son, he merely acquired the "name" of that which he already possessed, so noble and Christ-like was his character.[1]

We are led to conclude, therefore, that as strict as are Gregory's words to those who would delay baptism, his over-all view is one that allows for pre-Christian and post-Christian extra-sacramental "baptism." Salvation was not restricted solely to those who had undergone the church's specific rite. When Gregory says, then, that "heaven is common to all . . . and we are all recreated by the sufferings of Christ, not just these here and those there," he means to be taken seriously.[2] In harmony with such a view is his argument against the rigorism of Novatus, as he pleads for a greater exercise of philanthrōpia towards those who might otherwise be too harshly judged or condemned.[3] And there are these telling words from his little-known Oration, De moderatione in disputando:

> It is true that there is but one Lord, one faith, and one baptism . . . But can we equally say that there is but one road to salvation . . . and that those who turn away from it are strictly in error, rejected by God and excluded from the heavenly hope? Nothing would be more dangerous than to give such advice or to believe it on its own account![4]

A final question we must ask of Gregory's doctrine of the Holy Spirit and of baptism--a question we have already asked of his views on the economy of the Body of Christ--concerns the extent to which he believes the benefits received in baptism to be complete and/or permanent. Does baptism, in fact, insure the individual of a full realization of theōsis now, or, if not, does

---

1. Or. 18.6 (PG 35.992BC).
2. Or. 33.9 (PG 36.225B).
3. Or. 39.19 (PG 36.357BC).
4. Or. 32.33 (PG 36.212AB).

it guarantee that the path towards ultimate theōsis will be unhindered? Is baptism, as the "fulfillment of Christ's promise and of man's hope," the final stage in the economy of salvation?

We have already seen that there is no doubt in Gregory's mind as to the unequalled benefits of baptism by the Spirit. Baptism does effect a true change in the individual; it is the appropriate means by which one partakes of the salvation made universally available through the work of Christ. In the new creation, into which the baptized are re-born, death continues to exist, but its character and power have changed. To the baptized, death is no longer a threat to life, for it is only a temporary barrier separating us from an even fuller life. "I have no fear of death," Gregory has his friend Basil say in the face of threats made to him by the Prefect Modestus, "since death is my benefactor, sending me all the more quickly to God."[1] In the new creation, sin too continues to exist, but, as we have noted, baptism does away with past sins and provides us with the weapons to protect us from future sins. Sin, in fact, is "buried" in the waters of baptism.[2] And, in the new creation, the Evil One continues to attack the noble creation of humanity, failing to admit that he has already been beaten, and hoping to entrap the unwary. But baptism, says Gregory, gives us the means to ward off even his most subtle attacks. The Christian, for instance, has a ready reply to the Devil's demands that he worship him instead of God:

> Relying on the seal of baptism you can say to him: I am myself the image of God; unlike you, I have not yet been cast down from the glory above on account of my pride. I have put on Christ. I have been transformed into Christ through baptism. It is you who should worship me.[3]

---

1. Or. 43.49 (PG 36.560C). 2. Or. 40.4 (PG 36.364).
3. Ibid., 10 (PG 36.372A).

Much has been accomplished, then, for the individual in baptism. But has everything? "No, certainly
not," would be Gregory's answer were we to put this
question to him. Like the salvation wrought by Christ,
the benefits of baptism, as great as they are, are
neither mechanical nor instantaneous. There is, in
fact, nothing "indelible" about the gifts received at
baptism. These benefits are indeed a "gift," since
they are given in return for nothing; but, more than
this, baptism is also a "grace," since it is given
even--or, we should say, especially--to those who are
in debt.[1] Yet baptism is not an irrevocable or inerad-
icable promise of salvation or of theōsis. In keeping
with his views of creation and incarnation, Gregory
holds, in his understanding of the sacrament of baptism, to the important principle of growth. Accordingly, as in the old, so in the new creation, one is
called, not to a static existence, but to a dynamic
progress toward one's divinely ordained goal. Baptism
may be a gift, but it is not to be equated to the final
reward. Baptism may be the means of "escaping the fire,"
but it is not the necessary equivalent of the "inheritance of glory."[2] Baptism is a gift, says Gregory, but
a gift to be "cultivated."[3] And salvation, even after
baptism, is something that must be continuously worked
on (ἀεὶ δὲ τὴν σωτηρίαν ἐργάζου).[4] Baptism is not
something that can be "stolen" from Christ out of a
self-assured certainty of post-baptismal security.[5]
It is equally difficult, insists Gregory, to "obtain"
the blessings of baptism as it is to "retain" them.[6]
Baptism, in a word, erases past sins, but it holds no
automatic efficacy in respect to present and future
sins. Therefore, baptism involves a double struggle:
the preparation required before the sacrament itself

---

1. Or. 40.4 (PG 36.361D-364A).
2. Ibid., 12 (PG 36.373C).
3. Ibid., 22 (PG 36.389A).
4. Ibid., 14 (PG 36.376C).
5. Ibid., 33 (PG 36.405B).
6. Ibid., 31 (PG 36.401D).

is received, and the preparation required before one
undertakes to persevere in the benefits which baptism
effects.[1]

These statements, then, are clearly indicative of
Gregory's affirmation that the principles by which the
first creation were guided still hold true for the new.
The successive stages in the economy of salvation have
restored mankind the potential for fulfilling the
Godward pilgrimage, a potential lost when Adam suc-
cumbed to temptation and fell. But in the new creation,
entered into through the portal of baptism, neither
one's free will nor one's responsibility have been
obliterated. For Gregory, as we have seen, a salvation
which relies on force or restraint is no salvation;
free will and freedom (ἐξουσία , ἐλευθερία) are
necessary to the salvific process if one is to be
saved.[2]

When Gregory says that baptism is something to be
"cultivated," we are reminded of his image of the
crooked sapling. And indeed Gregory uses a similar
image when he says that the person who receives baptism is like the Canaanite woman who is "bent over"
under the weight of sin, but now, through re-birth,
has been made straight.[3] And, like the remedy applied
to the crooked sapling, the salvific effect of baptism

---

1. Or. 40.31 (PG 36.401D).
2. Stephan (op. cit., p. 11) has seen in Gregory's
statement that Christ "died in vain" for the Arians
(see above, p. 99) precisely this two-fold nature of
salvation (Christ's action and man's response) which
is so evident in Gregory's understanding of baptism:
"Also ist er doch auch für sie gestorben, aber ver-
gebens. Daraus erhellt zur Genüge, dass Gregor die
Grundlagen hat die später zur Unterscheidung führten
zwischen dem Erlösungswerk selbst und der Wirkung
desselben . . . zwischen der Erwerbung des Heiles
durch Christus und der Aneignung desselben durch die
Menschen, also einer objektiven (virtuellen-affektiven)
und einer subjektiven (aktuellen-effektiven) Erlösung.
3. Or. 40.33 (PG 36.405B).

is neither sudden nor violent. Rather than being an
earth-shaking κόσμου κατακλυσμός it is a resting
place on a long journey, an inn where the pilgrim may
stop, briefly, and then start out refreshed and full
of courage.[1] As the sacrifice of Christ was both the
"principle" and "beginning" of universal salvation,
so too baptism is the "principle" and "beginning" of
the individual's progress in the new creation towards
theōsis. But this salvation can never be taken for
granted; the journey still lies ahead. In the course
of this journey the Christian has it within his or
her created power to "undo" one's baptism, to "renounce" it.[2] Yet still ahead lies that future glory
of which baptism in the Spirit is but the foretype or
"outline."[3] Between the "here and now" of our individual appropriation of the universal victory wrought
by God in Christ and the "then and there" of mankind's
future inheritance lies the area of Gregory's concern
which might best be described as his concept of the
Christian life. Inherent in one's renewed potential
for growth is the ever-present danger of turning away
from God who created and preserves us, and whose
every care is for our salvation. Both the dangers
inherent in the Christian life as well as the indescribable joy of its possible fulfillment are found
in some of Gregory's more poignant lines of poetry,
of which the following, taken from his poem entitled
On Virtue, is a characteristic example:

---

1. Or. 40.7 (PG 36.368A).
2. Gregory points to the Emperor Julian as one who,
by his apostacy and subsequent lapse into paganism,
had repudiated his own baptism: Or. 5.52 (PG 35.576BC).
And in his dogmatic poem, De Spiritu Sancto, Gregory
speaks of the deity of the Spirit as that which purifies us in baptism, and then says: "If from this deity
I cut myself off, better it would be . . . yet I shud-
der at the thought of finishing my sentence."
1.1.3.47-9 (PG 37.411-2).
3. Or. 40.46 (PG 36.425A).

144

The soul that is not governed by the Word
Slips slowly downward in its dissipation.
But if it has His dominion and constant curb,
The Word will raise it up, and soon it will
Come to the heavenly city and there taste
Of things it has always longed for. For
    passing beyond
The veil and present shadows and the riddle
Of the world, here glimpsing Beauty as in
    a mirror,
It will then with pure mind see Goodness bare
And cease its wandering, sated by the light
It always longed for, possessing ultimate Good.[1]

So Gregory describes the joyful end of the Christian life. But before that end, the struggle is constant. It is to Gregory's multifaceted understanding of that struggle and its possibilities that we now turn.

---

1. 1.2.10.70-83 (PG 37.685-6); trans. Musurillo.

CHAPTER VII -- THE CHRISTIAN LIFE

In the tenth article of his "New Decalogue,"[1] Gregory says that the dogma outlined in the previous nine articles serves as the foundation of the Christian life, since faith apart from works is dead.[2] Here Gregory gives voice to the necessary but often overlooked principle that the basic motivation behind all of Christian ethics is dogmatics, that is, what the Christian does must take its direction from what God has done. The ethical imperative, in a word, stems from the divine indicative: the Christian should do this precisely because God has done that, and not vice versa. This is certainly Gregory's view, for he sees the salvific action of God in Christ as the fundamental pattern by which he can rule his own life. The necessary guideposts for one's ascent towards one's created, and now re-created, destiny of theōsis can be discovered only by reference to God's descent into the world of his creating. The divine model is the principle of the Christian life, although, needless to say, it is not identical with it. Or, as Gregory understands it, the Christian life is a mimēsis of those very steps undertaken by God to procure our salvation.

Gregory is characteristically unsystematic in the presentation of his ethical views, having written no sustained treatise on the subject. Rather, throughout his works, and chiefly in his poetry, there can be found hand in hand with his more dogmatic utterances a general approach to the Christian life which has distinct Gregorian traits.[3] Of these, two stand out as

---

1. Or. 40.45 (PG 36.424CD).
2. Ibid., (PG 36.424D); Jas. 2:17, 20.
3. So also Ruether (op. cit., p. 128): "Gregory of Nazianzus never wrote any systematic treatise on asceticism and contemplation. Hy hymned it in his poems; it fills his letters and his orations. He constantly

being the controlling motifs of his approach. The one
is solitary and God-directed, the other corporate and
neighbor-directed. The first is askēsis, the second
philanthrōpia, each of them imitative of the divine
oikonomia of salvation, and each of them, as we shall
see, playing a contributive role in that oikonomia. We
shall examine each in turn.

(1) Askēsis, as an ethical ideal, is the attempt
to imitate the asceticism of Christ. Its first and most
obvious expression is to be found in suffering, a suffering that comes about through humility and poverty,
through fasting and obedience, and finally through passion and death. Since this was the suffering asceticism
of Christ it is therefore the most recognizable mark of
the Christian life. Because Christ offered himself for
our sakes, says Gregory, let us "offer ourselves," and
thus "become for the sake of Christ all that he became
for our sake."[1] It is by living "according to Christ,"
Gregory tells his congregation, that they "become
Christs."[2] And the greatest praise that Gregory has
for the Apostle Paul is that he was an "imitator" of
Christ who was willing, after Christ, "to suffer anything."[3] To this ascetic imitation there are no limits;
it may even include the "sacrifice of ourselves":

> Let us accept anything for the sake of the
> Word. By our sufferings, let us imitate
> his suffering; by our blood, let us digni-
> fy his blood. The nails are sweet, even
> though painful. For to suffer for and with

---

tried to live by its tenets, but he never wrote an
organized account of its principles. His doctrine on
the subject must be extracted from bits and pieces
scattered through his writings." This has, in fact,
been done by T. Spidlik (op. cit.) in his work on
Gregory's spirituality, and to a lesser extent by J.
Rousse in "Grégoire de Nazianze (saint)," in DSpir,
7, 932-71.

1. Or. 1.4, 5 (PG 35.397B-400A).
2. Or. 21.10 (PG 35.1092C).
3. Or. 2.55 (PG 35.465B).

Christ is more to be desired than a life
of ease with others.[1]

Or, as Gregory puts it elsewhere, against all possible
threats to one's life "there is but one cure, one road
to victory: I will glory in Christ, and in death for
Christ's sake."[2]
It is important to note that, for Gregory, suffering has no moral value in and of itself. Only as it is
imitative of the suffering of Christ can it be called
true askesis. Only as it is an imitatio Christi can it
be the means of participating in the victory which
Christ effected by his suffering and death. The Christian's suffering and death is symbolized in baptism
and experienced in martyrdom or self-sacrifice, and becomes, at the same time, a participation in the resurrection of Christ. Gregory is quite specific about this:
the necessity of being buried with Christ so as to rise
with him is related not only to the symbolic initiation
of baptism but also to the whole of the Christian's ongoing life.[3] Yet Gregory does not mean that an imitation
of Christ's passion and death need be taken literally;
ascetic suffering does not always lead to a literal
cross. Martyrdom, indeed, is praiseworthy; it is a
noble ideal. Every Christian, given the turmoil of the
world, may be called upon to witness unto death, and,
says Gregory, no one would at such a time wish to deny
one's faith or betray one's vocation through cowardice.
But, he counsels, martyrdom should be accepted only
when it is thrust upon one; it should never actively be
sought. No one should rush blindly or unadvisedly into
danger.[4] For this reason Gregory can at one and the
same time praise the martyr who meets a victorious although untimely end and praise, too, the ascetic whose

---

1. Or. 45.23 (PG 36.656B).
2. Or. 2.87 (PG 35.492A).
3. See Or. 7.23 (PG 35.785B).
4. Ibid., 14 (PG 35.772B).

149

long life of devotion ends in death by natural causes.[1]
Imitation of Christ's death may, for the Christian, take
the shape of actual physical death, or it may be a question of "crucifying oneself to the world and the world
to oneself."[2]

That the moral value of suffering is not found in
the suffering itself can also be seen in the purpose
which Gregory assigns to suffering, a purpose which is
perhaps best described as kathartic. The Christian endeavors through ascetic imitation to "ascend" from the
pressures and ties of an existence within the "storm of
life" so as to be the more perfectly able to comprehend
one's true destiny, to know and to be with God. It is at
this point that the most obvious element of askēsis,
that of suffering, becomes blended with its counterpart,
contemplation or theōria. In one passage Gregory equates
piety (εὐσέβεια) with the knowledge of one's origin, of
one's destiny, and of one's nature.[3] Askēsis, then, becomes more than suffering, more than being buried with
Christ so as to rise with him. It becomes also the im-
plementation of that knowledge which ever draws the
Christian closer to God. In other words, if imitative
asceticism has as its primary purpose the furthering of
one's ascent towards a life untroubled by worldly cares
or passions, it has also, as a parallel purpose, the
realization of the contemplative life, or as we have
described it earlier, the "philosophic" life. We have
also made mention of Gregory's abiding desire to escape from the world to some secluded haven where he
could, in peaceful solitude, meditate upon the glory
of the triune Godhead. This contemplative ideal, as we
saw, is analogous to the vision of God perceived by
Moses on Sinai. Gregory himself yearns for the same
vision and conceives of the progressive katharsis at-
tained through ascetic endeavor as the means of ascend-

---

1. See, for instance, Gregory's panegyric on the
Maccabees (Or. 15) and his encomium on his sister Gorgonia (Or. 8).
2. Or. 2.56 (PG 35.465B).
3. Or. 8.6 (PG 35.796B).

ing to that "mountain retreat" where the untroubled
pursuit of philosophia may lead him further into the
cloud of the divine mystery.[1] This need for an ascetic
purification before one can rise to the philosophical
life is expressed clearly by Gregory as follows:

> I know the height of God and the weakness
> of man as well as his power. Heaven is
> high and earth is deep, and who of those
> who have been cast down by sin shall as-
> cend? Who that is still surrounded by
> the darkness here below or the heaviness
> of the flesh will behold purely, with
> his whole mind, the whole Mind, and,
> amid visible and transitory things as-
> sociate with invisible and intransitory
> things?[2]

(2) The God-directed dimension of the Christian
life, for Gregory, is best described, then, as that
kind of askēsis which consists both of suffering, in
imitation of Christ, and of contemplation, in pursuit
of the knowledge of God. But a second and equally important dimension of the Christian life, which is
directed principally towards others, is the ethical
ideal of philanthrōpia. Whereas askēsis emphasizes
the solitary or monachistic ethic, philanthrōpia is
corporate or communal in its approach. And the former,
it would seem, is the necessary preparation for the
latter. We have referred to several passages already
in which Gregory writes as though he were a fugitive
from the world, concerned solely with individual as-

---

1. Or. 2.7 (PG 35.413C-416A), Or. 21.2 (PG 35.
1084D), Or. 28.2 (PG 36.28AB).
2. Or. 2.74 (PG 35.481B). A full discussion of Gregory's understanding of the ascetic and contemplative
life is given by H. Pinault, Le Platonisme de Saint
Grégoire de Nazianze (Le Roche-sur-Yon, 1925), pp.
113ff; see also Spidlik, op. cit., especially pp.
57ff.

cetic achievement. But these passages are off-set by his parallel conviction that such asceticism is the necessary prelude to the pastoral oversight of his congregation:

> Before one has, as far as possible risen
> superior to the passions , has sufficiently
> purified his mind, and has passed others
> in nearness to God, I do not see how one
> could expect to undertake the rule over
> souls or the role of mediator between man
> and God, for this, I believe, is what a
> priest is.[1]

Asceticism, therefore, is not an end in itself. There can be no question that Gregory's preference is for the solitary and contemplative life, but at the same time he can never finally refuse to accept the responsibility he feels towards others. Asceticism may be, for him, the ideal, but pastoral oversight, as an expression of philanthrōpia, is a necessity. He describes the bishop of Alexandria as one who had mediated between the solitary and communal life, and as one who demonstrated that the priesthood has its "philosophical" dimension as well as its "pastoral." Praxis and theōria, continues Gregory, were, in the life of Athanasius, effectively combined.[2]

---

1. Or. 2.91 (PG 35.493C). It is in this passage (and in 2.16) that we find the origin of that phrase which was to become so often used in medieval pastoral handbooks, beginning with the Gregory the Great's Liber Regulae Pastoralis, i.e., ars artium est regimen animarum. On the role of the priest as mediator, see M. Serra, "La carità pastorale in S. Gregorio Nazianzeno," OCP, 21 (1955), pp. 361-79.
2. Or. 21.19-20 (PG 35.1104AB). L. Bouyer (op. cit., p. 413) has described Gregory's monachism as "le seul désir d'une entière fidélité au Christ, d'une rupture décisive avec tout ce que pourrait nous séparer de lui." No mention, however, of the pastoral dimension.

Yet philanthrōpia, as an ethical ideal, is not con-
fined to the pastoral exercise of priesthood; it is enjoined upon all Christians. And here the motif of imitatio is as predominant as when Gregory speaks of the
ascetic life. Whereas askēsis may be described as the
mode of God's salvific action in Christ, philanthrōpia
is an imitation of its direction, i.e., towards mankind. A routine imitation of Christ's life and death
that does not also include the universal purpose for
which that life and death were undertaken is, for Gregory, completely meaningless. An ascetic ideal which
does not find expression in concern for others, which
"passes by" the man who fell among thieves, is not a
Christian ideal.[1] A catharsis of mind, soul, and body
that is not also translated into philanthropic works
is not a "purification," but a "defilement."[2] Gregory
is quite specific on this point; to neglect the poor
or the hungry, the homeless or the stranger, the sick
or the naked, amounts to the neglect of one's own salvation.[3] The "security," in fact, of one's body and
soul depends upon one's philanthrōpia.[4]

The comprehensive pattern for the redeemed life
which Christ provides resides in its being the expression of God's mercy towards mankind. Accordingly, Gregory urges his congregation to have God's own love
in themselves, to "be as God to the unfortunate, imitating the mercy of God, for in no way does man approach God so nearly as when he does good to his
neighbor ."[6]

---

1. Or. 14.37 (PG 35.908AB).
2. Ibid. (PG 35.908B).
3. Or. 40.31 (PG 36.401D-404C).
4. Or. 14.8 (PG 35.868B).
5. Ibid., 9 (PG 35.868C).
6. Ibid., 26-7 (PG 35.892C-893A). Gregory elsewhere
describes this imitative "philanthropy" as exemplified
in his sister Gorgonia by claiming that she "often,
through her efforts on the behalf of others, welcomed
Christ himself." Or. 8.12 (PG 35.804A). A. D. Nock has
commented upon this theme of imitating the mercy of

When Gregory thus speaks of one's "approach to God" by way of imitating his mercy, it comes as no surprise when we discover that basic to his whole understanding of the Christian life, whether ascetic or philanthropic, is his ever-present concern with theōsis as the goal of life. Only when we examine Gregory's various pronouncements on ethics within their soteriological context does this principle become manifest.

Within the ascetic dimension of the Christian life, for instance, we find manifold references to theōsis. If the asceticism of the Christian is an imitation of the asceticism of Christ, or a response to God's descent in Christ, its purpose, as we have seen, is so to participate in that divine event that the quality (static) of that life, as well as its direction (dynamic), are best described in terms of the ultimate destiny to which one is called, namely, theōsis. Christian asceticism is, in fact, an instrument of salvation, or at least an instrument of appropriating that salvation made universally available in Christ and individually available in baptism. This is as true of God-directed solitary asceticism as it is of neighbor-directed communal philanthropy, as can be demonstrated from many passages. To escape, by means of theōria, from the world of sense, and to be with God, asserts Gregory, is to ascend to that realm where theōsis is conferred by philosophia.[1] Those who rise superior to earthly phenomena, mortifying the flesh, "know no limit either in ἀνάβασιϛ or in θέω-σιϛ,"[2] that is, their "upwards" progress is unhinder-

_____

God in his "Notes on Ruler-Cult, I-IV," JHS, 48 (L928), p. 31, and also in his review of H. Meecham's The Epistole to Diognetus (Manchester, 1949), in JR, 31 (1951), pp. 214ff.

1. Or. 21.2 (PG 35.1084C).

2. Or. 4.71 (PG 35.593AB). C. W. King, who has translated Gregory's two invectives against Julian, shows little sympathy for Gregory's praise of Christian asceticism. Remarking on the passage here cited,

ed. Again, those who purify their bodies through fasting are "deified";[1] the anchorite living apart from
the world has "deified the mind."[2] Gregory also praises
those ascetics who have "hastened to leave the world so
that they might θεόſ εἶναι, who bear Christ in themselves, who honor the cross, . . . who contemplate God,
to whom God belongs and who belong to God."[3]

So too with Gregory's description of the philanthropic ideal. He speaks, for instance, of his solitary
life before ordination as one in which he was "coadju-
tor and mother of divine ascent, and deifier,"[4] but
after having been torn away from his preferred monachism, and having reluctantly accepted the priestly
office, he sees theōsis no longer as a personal goal
just for himself but as the goal of his ministry to
others. With these words he delineates the nature of
the pastoral art:

> My task is to furnish the soul with wings,
> to rescue it from the world, to give it to
> God, . . . and to make Christ dwell in the
> heart by the Spirit, in short, to deify
> (θεὸν ποιῆσαι), and bestow heavenly beati-
> tude on those whose true home is above.[5]

With similar words he underlines the ascetic prepara-

---

he suggests that Gregory's audience was "too obtuse to
perceive the difference between Julian's contempt for
luxury practised for the real good of the empire and
the asceticism of the monks and hermits, tending to
their own glorification and uselessness." Julian the
Emperor (London, 1888), loc. cit.

1. 1.2.10.630-1 (PG 37.725-6).
2. 1.2.17.1-2 (PG 37.781). One can but wonder what
led the translator of the Benedictine edition of Gregory's poetry to render this phrase, ". . . et mentem
tollit ad astra suam." (!)
3. 1.2.1.210-4 (PG 37.538).
4. Or. 3.1 (PG 35.517A).
5. Or. 2.22 (PG 35.432B), and similar passages
throughout this Oration.

tion necessary for the priesthood:

> The priest must first . . . become light
> and then illumine others, draw near to God
> and then lead others near, be hallowed and
> then hallow others. . . . He must share the
> priesthood of Christ . . . and, greatest of
> all, become God and deify others.[1]

In like fashion Gregory assigns to the philanthropic
ideal the purpose of imitating the salvific philanthrōpia of God. He makes this clear when he defines "love"
towards others as the "road to God, the way of theōsis."[2] "Imitate the mercy of God," he says with even
greater emphasis, "for the most divine attribute that
man has is to do good. It is possible, with no special
effort on your part to become God; don't throw away
the opportunity for your deification."[3]

Gregory's concept of the Christian life, then, has
as its two major themes the ascetic endeavor on the one
hand and the philanthropic response on the other. Each
is a participation in, and imitation of, the salvific

---

1. Ibid., 71, 73 (PG 35.480B, 481B). Gregory describes his friend Basil's ministry in like manner, referring to those of his congregation whom he has "deified and exalted." Ep. 6 (PG 37.29C).

2. 1.2.34.160-1 (PG 37.957).

3. Or. 17.9 (PG 35.976CD). The apparent contradiction between contributing to one's own salvation and
becoming God "with no special effort" on one's own
part is resolved in the latter part of this passage
where we discover that Gregory is not asking his congregation to perform heroic acts of virtue, such as
those attributed to Abraham, but to develop an attitude of charity towards others, an attitude consistent
with God's mercy but not necessarily requiring a superabundant measure of "pain." Elsewhere, of course, as
we have already seen, Gregory is more strenuous in his
demand for a high degree of ascetic endeavor, no less
for himself than for others.

156

action of God in Christ. Each safeguards and furthers
the perfection of the re-created order into which the
individual Christian has been reborn. Each, therefore,
advances the individual's ascent towards the divinely
ordained destiny of theōsis. But a serious question
comes to mind at this point, a question that we can by
no means avoid. It is a question, also, which comes
rather quickly to the lips of Westerners as they seek
to interpret the thought of an Easterner. If we are
faithful to Gregory, however, we must both ask the
question and, in spite of our quasi-Augustinian preju-
dices, look for an answer. Given Gregory's conviction
that universal salvation has been wrought in the economy of the incarnation, and that this salvation is
appropriated primarily in baptism by the economy of
the Holy Spirit; given further Gregory's assertion
that the individual has the responsibility of safe-
guarding this salvation since it can be undone by
spiritual negligence, to what extent does Gregory believe one's salvation to depend, in the final analysis,
on one's own "works" of ascetic and philanthropic imitation? Does Gregory, in fact, conceive of the realization of ultimate theōsis, albeit based upon the
work of God, as dependent in the long run on our
work? Does he not portray salvation, to put it more
directly, as a "reward" rather than as a "gift"?
    To reach an answer to this question, we must exa-
mine Gregory's understanding of the relation between
God's grace and human free will. We have already
pointed out that Gregory attributed our created free
will to the principle that, within the economy of salvation, our progress or ascent towards theōsis must,
if it is to have any value, be the result of voluntary choice and not of coercion. We indicated further
that Gregory conceived of this progress as a creative struggle between body and soul, a struggle that
is mutually pedagogical and aims at the growth of
the whole person. Even in the recreated order this struggle continues, although, with the presence of sin and
mortality, it is a multidimensional struggle. Sin and
mortality have been conquered, in principle; salvation has been achieved, in principle. But because there

is nothing mechanical or instantaneous about either, one must, by virtue of the created principle of growth, participate actively in one's own salvation. It is important to recognize the explicit manner in which Gregory makes this assertion. Our final attainment of salvation or theōsis is not solely a "gift of God"; it is also a "prize for virtue."[1] God's work is not here opposed to our work; they are both mutually operative in the economy of salvation. It is not a question of grace or free will, but of grace and free will.

Gregory is quite insistent in his refusal to belittle the salvific importance of our ethical response to God's action in Christ. He defines the Christian ascetic, for instance, as one who strives constantly for increasing virtue "until that end and deification" for which he was born, towards which he presses, hopeful of a reward commensurate with God's magnanimity."[2] Theōsis, quite precisely, is a "prize,"[3] and salvation can be "purchased" by moral effort.[4]

Such statements will strike most of those who have been raised in the tradition of Augustinian "orthodoxy" as blatantly Pelagian. Yet the issues that were to separate the Doctor gratiae from his Welsh adversary were issues that would strike no responsive chord in the Fathers of the East. Their basic presuppositions and theological categories were, on this point, totally different from those of the West.[5] Only when we realize this can we appreciate the constant vigor with

---

1. Or. 2.17 (PG 35.425C); see Spidlik, op. cit., p. 72.
2. Or. 4.124 (PG 35.664C).
3. Ep. 178 (PG 37.293A).
4. Or. 45.24 (PG 35.656C). See also Or. 40.12 (PG 36.373C) and 1.1.33.222 (PG 37.944). Szymusiak (op. cit., p. 35, n. 45) speaks of this combination of free will and grace as follows: "Il est tout à fait digne de la suprême bonté de faire nôtre le bien qui se trouve non seulement départi à la nature mais élaboré par notre libre aribtre."
5. See, for instance, H. A. Wolfson, "St. Augustine

which Gregory insists on the ascetic and philanthropic ideal as the means of combatting fatalism on the one hand and arbitrary election on the other.[1] Reflecting on Paul's assertion that God's mercy depends neither on our will nor on our personal effort, and referring also to the request of the sons of Zebedee,[2] Gregory asks:

> Is the ruling of our minds nothing? Nothing our effort? Nothing our reason? Are philosophical pursuits nothing? Nothing our fasting, our sleepless vigils, our hard pallets, our shedding of tears? Are all these to no avail?

If Gregory is thus unwilling to belittle or undercut the role of one's moral effort in the plan of salvation; if, for instance, he can praise one's "natural" aptitudes but sees those virtues arrived at by stint of moral exertion as even more praiseworthy,[4] this should by no means lead us to assume that he thereby denigrates the grace of God. The validity of "works" rests on God's original gracious purposes in creating us with free will so that we could contribute to our own salvation. But that very free will was a created gift, a token of the merciful grace of God. According-

---

and the Pelagian Controversy," in Religious Philosophy: A Group of Essays (Cambridge, Mass., 1961), pp. 158-76. Lot-Borodine, who more than once has sought to divorce Eastern patristic thought from Western misinterpretations, asserts for some uncharacteristic reason that the Greek concept of grace is equivalent to the late medieval nominalistic adage: "Faciendi quod in se est, Deus non denegat gratiam suam." (Op. cit., Vol. 106, p. 543). See Harnack, DG, 3, pp. 266f.
  1. See Symusiak, op. cit., pp. 35-8.
  2. Rom. 9:16, Mat. 20:20ff.
  3. Or. 37.14 (PG 36.300C).
  4. Ibid., 16 (PG 36.301AB).

ly, Gregory insists that ascetic or philanthropic effort, apart from the initial and sustaining grace of God, is impossible. In speaking, for instance, of the katharsis begun in baptism, he says that it is Christ who effects (ἐνεργέω) it.[1] In praising the martyrs, he claims that it is Christ who arms (ἐξοπλίζω) the "athlete" with his own sufferings.[2] Christians, as we have seen, must themselves be the source of their own perseverance, but, adds Gregory, without Christ one is no more able to progress towards one's final goal than a bird can fly without air or a fish swim without water.[3] In a poem where Gregory outlines the guideposts for the Christian life, hoping himself to follow them, he concludes that "if, by this desire, I reach my goal, it will be because of thy grace (χάρισμα), O Eternal One."[4] A similar statement is made in yet another poem where Gregory determines to adopt a regula vitae, but recognizing that his ability to follow it depends on his having "Christ for my help, my companion, and my guide."[5] And, as often as Gregory urges his congregation to pursue the path of virtue, he also adds that "even to wish well requires help (βοήθεια) from God."[6]

---

1. Or. 39.1 (PG 36.336A). See also Pinault, op. cit., pp. 146-8.

2. Or. 7.12 (PG 35.769B). The idea of Christ suffering in and for martyrs is a familiar theme in early Christian literature. See, for instance, Felicitas' statement when, having given birth in prison to a child, she is asked by her jailor what she will do, if she cries out so in childbirth, when she meets with the beasts in the arena: "Modo ego patior quod patior; illic autem alius erit in me qui patietur pro me." Passio Sanct. Perpet. et Felic., 15 (Ed. Kruger). See also F. M. Young, "A Reconsideration of Alexandrian Christology." JEH, 22 (1971), pp. 103-14.

3. 1.2.9.103-6 (PG 37.675-6).

4. 2.1.2.20-30 (PG 37.1019).

5. 2.2.4.80-2 (PG 37.1511).

6. Or. 37.13 (PG 36.297C).

What emerges, therefore, from Gregory's writings is a conception of the Christian life in which salvation by "works" and salvation by "grace" are not opposites but the obverse sides of a single reality. Gregory himself states that he is attempting to achieve a balance between what is natural to him and what he freely chooses, i.e., between what is given him and what he himself achieves.[1] Only thus can salvation be both a "gift" and a "reward," of human and divine source. Or, as Gregory puts it, salvation is not just a question of "to whom it is given," nor only a question of "to those who are worthy," but a question of combining the two.[2] Grace without moral response is, for Gregory, meaningless, and free moral response without grace is impossible.

This concept of the mutual relation between "gift" and "reward," as it appears in the Greek Fathers, is described by Henry Chadwick in an apt metaphor. The redeemed, he says, do not move towards their destiny by necessity; the steps to heaven are a "stairway" for them to climb, not an "escalator" for them to ride.[3] Rosemary Ruether has also put it well. "Gregory," she writes, "does not fall into the tendency either to attribute all to man, or to attribute a part to man and a part to God, but he can simultaneously say that man's salvation is his own work and also that it is entirely the work of God. . . Man receives in proportion as he strives, and strives through the power of God that he receives."[4]

Gregory's characteristically Eastern emphasis on the Christian's progress towards theōsis being the result of both divine aid and human endeavor is further

---

1. Ibid., 20 (PG 36.305BC).
2. Ibid., 13 (PG 36.297B). Elsewhere Gregory expresses this combination of "grace" and "works" by saying, "Do not be ignorant of the measure of grace, nor let the enemy sow tares while you are asleep!" Or. 40.34 (PG 36.408C).
3. Chadwick, op. cit., p. 119.
4. Ruether, op. cit., pp. 137f.

exemplified by his insistence on the need for penitence. At this point Gregory is quite realistic; he places seemingly unrealizable demands for perfection both on himself and on others, but at the same time admits that no one--he least of all--can ultimately meet these demands. He recognizes, in a word, the discrepancy between his vocation to become increasingly "godlike" and his very "ungodlike" failures; he confesses the contradiction between the Christian's claim to be a "new creation" through baptism and the sinful nature retained even after baptism. As Samuel Laeuchli has phrased it: "The Christian message spoke of a new life, or even of 'deification,' and the person baptized was called a new being. But he was not! The redeemed did not differ from the unredeemed in their moral life ."[1] Just as the effects of baptism are, for Gregory, not necessarily permanent, so too there is and can be no stage on the progressive path towards theōsis where the Christian can claim his journey to be complete. Gregory's realism with respect to our abiding creatureliness and sinfulness begins with his open willingness himself to be the "first" among his congregation to confess his sins. Further, as E. Michaud has demonstrated, Gregory's realism includes his confession that the church as a whole is still far from being perfect.[2] Let no one be so proud as to think himself to be pure, admonishes Gregory.[3] Only as we recognize our own sin, he continues, can we be forgiven; and similarly, only as we forgive others shall we ourselves find forgiveness.[4]

---

1. S. Laeuchli, The Serpent and the Dove: Five Essays in Early Christianity (New York/Nashville, 1966), p. 186.

2. E. Michaud, "Ecclésiologie de St. Grégoire de Nazianze," RIT, 12 (1904), pp. 557-73. But cf. J. Karmiri's idealistic portrayal of Gregory's views here in Ἐκ τῆς ἐκκλησιολογίας τοῦ ἁγίου Γρεγορίου τοῦ θεολόλου, Ekkl, 36 (1959), pp. 305-8.

3. Or. 39.19 (PG 36.357BC).

4. Or. 16.14-15 (PG 35.952D-956B), Or. 40.31 (PG 36.404B), and Ep. 77 (PG 37.145A).

Gregory does not discuss penitence systematically; nor does he mention penance within an ecclesiastical or sacramental framework.[1] He describes it rather as a constant attitude of the Christian, an attitude of humility. There are occasional references to the Eucharist as the sacramental means of receiving forgiveness for post-baptismal sins,[2] and in one passage Gregory speaks of the Last Supper as that sacramental meal which "destroys" the darkness of sin."[3] But aside from these scattered references to penitential discipline or to the absolution available in the Eucharist, Gregory's concern is more with a general call to a penitential life than with the specific instrumentalities by which forgiveness may be obtained. In this context, he wishes neither to presume on the grace of God nor on human ability. The need for forgiveness is constant, since only to God does it belong not to sin; and that forgiveness is constantly available, since God's chief abiding attribute is that of mercy.[4] This constant need for forgiveness is enigmatically underlined when Gregory asserts that, although God does tend to gentleness and away from wrath, yet he still does not forgive sinners absolutely lest, through any over-reliance on his mercy, they should grow worse.[5]

The "storm of life," then, in which Gregory feels so embroiled, continues from the economy of creation, with its creative struggle between body and soul, through to the life of the redeemed in the "new creation." Gregory exhibits such anxiety, at times, about the difficulty of living as he knows he ought, that he might, with some justification, be accused of repeating the Adamic

---

1. He does, however, refer to the various "ranks" of penitents in Or. 39.13 (PG 36.357B).
2. As in Ep. 171 (PG 37.280C). For the "curative" power of the Eucharist, see Or. 8.18 (PG 35.809B-812A) and Or. 18.38 (PG 35.1036C); for the "deificatory" power of the Eucharist, see Or. 25.2 (PG 35.1200BC).
3. Or. 45.16 (PG 36.644C).
4. Or. 16.14-15 (PG 35.953AB).
5. Or. 18.25 (PG 35.1013C).

sin of impatience by prematurely reaching out for his
destiny. Only too well he knows the vicissitudes of
life in this world; he can even envy those whose death
has brought them respite from the struggle.[1] Yet, as
harsh a training ground as is life in the flesh, it is
a necessary one, and when Gregory is not too over-con-
cerned about its harshness, he accepts its necessity
with vigor and determination. As a pastor having responsibility for the destiny of his flock, he sees his
role as that of a "sponsor" of God's philanthrōpia, as
the "mediator," for his people, between God's wrath
and his mercy.[2] He is anxious, therefore, not only for
himself, but for those committed to his charge, exer-
cising his office on their behalf so that, when they
stand before God on the final judgement day, they may
enter into the inheritance of eternal praise because
of their virtue, and not into the inheritance of eternal punishment because of their vice.[3]

Gregory does not speculate as to when this final
judgment will take place, and gives no indication of
either apocalyptic or chiliastic tendencies. He limits
his remarks to a statement which we have already had
occasion to cite, namely, that the "end" will come
when all that Christ has been sent to do is accomplished.[4] The only reference to an eschatological "time-
table" is his mentioning that, after death, the soul
goes to await its final disposition, and a "little later" the body too will rise.[5]

But although Gregory is imprecise as to the specif-
ics of the end, he writes with considerable conviction
as to the general meaning of the final judgment. It
will be a judgment, he says, of one's faith and works,
taking place after the general resurrection, and will
effect the separation of the "saved" from the "lost."[6]

---

1. As in Or. 7.20 (PG 35.780BC).
2. Or. 16.14 (PG 35.953A).
3. Or. 2.28 (PG 35.437A).
4. Or. 30.14 (PG 36.121C), Or. 40.45 (PG 36.421C).
5. Or. 7.21 (PG 35.781C).
6. Or. 30.4 (PG 36.108C).

Because of the "finality" of the final judgment, Gregory warns that:

> It is better to be corrected and purified
> now than to be delivered over to that fu-
> ture chastisement when there will be pun-
> ishment, not purification. For . . . in
> hell there is no confession or restora-
> tion for those who have departed. For God
> has limited man's life and practise to
> this world, and the inquiry into them to
> the next.[1]

Gregory makes this explicit denial of an Origenis-
tically understood universalism even clearer when he
asserts that:

> Those who have done good will go to the
> resurrection of life which is now hidden
> in Christ but which will later be made
> manifest with him; but those who have done
> evil will go to the resurrection of judg-
> ment to which those who have not believed
> have already been condemned by the Word
> which judges them. The former will be tak-
> en up into unspeakable light and will be-
> hold the holy and royal Trinity . . .
> while the latter will be banished from
> God and bear in their conscience a shame
> that has no end.[2]

These words, it must be remembered, are addressed to
Christians, so Gregory's reference to "those who have
not believed" is not to "pagans" but to apostates or
impenitent members of the church. Gregory even suggests that pagans will be judged less harshly than
Christians since they are not bound by Christian or-
dinances and have therefore less moral responsibility

---

1. Or. 16.7 (PG 35.944BC).
2. Ibid., 9 (PG 35.945).

than do the baptized.[1] Gregory will still, however, use threats to induce the unbaptized to enter into the circle of the redeemed, but his strongest threats are directed against those who have already been baptized in order to warn them of the dire consequences which their post-baptismal sins may invite, consequences even more dire than if they had not been baptized at all:

> Do not become dead again and live like those who live in the tombs, nor bind yourselves again with the chains of your own sins. It is not certain whether you will rise from the tombs again,[2] until that final and general resurrection which will bring every work under judgment, not to be healed but to be judged, and to render account for the good or evil that has been stored up.[3]

Gregory leaves little doubt as to the seriousness of his concept of the final judgment when he insists that the punishment due the wicked is ἀθάνατος, and that the fire to which the Devil and his angels, as well as those who have done evil, will go is διαιω-νίζων.[4] Yet, for all the strength of such assertions, Gregory is finally unwilling to be overly categorical in respect to judgment, and tempers his view of eternal damnation by suggesting that there may be a fire that is more worthy of divine justice and more merciful than the eternal fire of unending punishment.[5]

---

1. 2.28.267-8 (PG 37.876).
2. It is not clear what Gregory means here by "rising from the tombs" before the general resurrection, since his more demonstrable view, as we shall see, is that the body remains in the tomb until the very last day.
3. Or. 40.33 (PG 36.405C-408A).
4. Or. 2.28 (PG 35.437A) and Or. 40.36 (PG 36.412A).
5. Or. 16.7 (PG 35.944BC).

Still, Gregory never pursues this point, and we would
be unwise to make too much of it. In one of his autobiographical poems, for instance, he does raise the
question as to whether at some future date all will
return to God, but evades the issue by answering with
a terse "this is not the place to discuss such a matter."[1] We cannot, however, in spite of such statements,
conclude, as some have, that Gregory is here making a
veiled concession to Origenistic universalism, or that
his eschatological views parallel those of Gregory of
Nyssa.[2]

What we can conclude, however, is that, seen against
the background of the interdependence of grace and free
will, Gregory's views are characterized by an unwilling-
ness to define too sharply the assertions he makes. His
demand for imitative askēsis and philanthrōpia is closely balanced by his confession of the constant need for
divine grace, while the apparent finality of his eschatological declarations is balanced by his conviction
that for mankind there is a never-ending potential for
growth towards theōsis. Although the "economy of the
flesh" has come to an end, says Gregory, and although
Christ has ascended into heaven, he is still the one
Mediator who "even now intercedes, as man, for my salvation, for he continues in the body which he assumed
until he makes me God by the power of the incarnation."[3]
Gregory's attitude towards ultimate salvation, then,
is marked more by hope than by fear. Accordingly, when
he speaks of the "last things," he alludes once more
to the "gentleness" of the final earthquake. Even to
the last, God will not use coercion. "O maker and trans-
former in due time of all things by the Creator Word,"
prays Gregory, ". . . receive us when we die prepared
through thy fear, and neither troubled nor withdrawn

---

1. 2.1.1.546 (PG 37.1010).
2. Turmel ("L'eschatologie," p. 106ff) claims Gregory's views to be an imitation of Origen, and Kelly,
(Early Christian Doctrines, p. 483) postulates a similarity between the Nazianzen and Gregory of Nyssa.
3. Or. 30.14 (PG 36.121C).

[from] thee at the last day, nor dragged away from our life here by force . . . but filled with eagerness for that blessed and lasting life which is in Christ Jesus our Lord."[1]

The image of the crooked sapling which we encountered earlier continues to play its role, albeit unconsciously, in Gregory's thought. In one of his letters to Theodore of Tyana, for instance, Gregory suggests that gentle restraint and kindness are far more effective as cures for sinful waywardness than harsh threats or even blows. Then (side-stepping the implications of Jesus' action before the fig-tree)[2] he goes on to say:

> Let us not then dry up a fig-tree that may
> yet bear fruit; let us not condemn it as
> useless or as taking up too much ground,
> since perhaps the care and diligence of a
> skillful gardener may yet restore it.[3]

Constant and continual growth, these are the marks of our gradual ascent towards theōsis as they are of the Christian life as a whole, even to the end. Whether defined in terms of solitary God-directed asceticism or of communal neighbor-directed philanthropy, Gregory's fundamental concern remains soteriological. Theōsis is both the principle of our growth and the destiny towards which we grow. Theōsis, in the Christian life, is the human response to the divine enanthrōpēsis. That this is so can be seen clearly in one of Gregory's few references to the Last Supper:

> And Jesus himself, in the upper room,
> communicated to those who were being
> initiated into the highest aspects of
> the mystery, so that it might be shown
> that it is necessary for God to come

---

1. Or. 7.24 (PG 35.788BC).
2. Mat. 11:12ff. Gregory, it seems, prefers the "parable" of the fig-tree in Lk. 13:6-9.
3. Ep. 77 (PG 37.145B).

down to us . . . and that we must go up
to God, and in such wise there will be
communion of God with men.[1]

Because Gregory has unbounded confidence that such a
human-divine "communion" has been established, beginning in God's gracious act of creation, and continuing
throughout the whole of the economy of salvation, he
never loses sight of his future goal. The final dwell-
ing place (κατοικία), he says, is certainly better than
the journey (παροικία) one takes to reach it.[2] Nevertheless, the journey itself is always the medium of
opportunity for growth:

[Let us] sow unto righteousness and reap
the fruit of life (for πρᾶξιʃ is the co-
adjutor of θεωρία) so that we learn,
among other things, what is the true
light and what is the false. . . Let us
become lights in the world, holding
forth to others the word of life, that
is, the life-giving power. . . Let us
journey towards his light.[3]

This balance between our final destiny and the
"stormy" path required to reach it is aptly phrased
in a characteristically Gregorian couplet:

Christ for me the reward of everything is,
And the poverty of his cross I carry as
    riches.[4]

Here we can see that Gregory's concept of the present life of the Christian finds its ultimate meaning
and definition only in reference to the goal towards
which that life is directed. The future, in a word,

---

1. Or. 41.12 (PG 36.445B).
2. Or. 18.3 (PG 35.988D).
3. Or. 40.37 (PG 36.412C).
4. 1.2.10.465-6 (PG 37.714).

informs the meaning of the present. The whole of the Christian's response to the salvation wrought by God in Christ is to progress, through an imitation of the very principles whereby that salvation has been effected, more and more towards one's final destiny, towards one's celestial habitation. With Christ as his guide and companion on the path, Gregory yearns for that final state. He describes it as a time when:

> No longer from afar will I behold the truth,
> As if in a mirror reflected on the water's
>   surface.
> Rather, the truth itself will I see with
>   eyes unveiled,
> The truth whose first and primary mark the
>   Trinity is,
> God as one adored, a single light in
>   tri-equal beams.[1]

Which statement, in effect, brings us back to where this study began, namely, that the theological quest will be realized, our search for God will end, only through the gradual process of theōsis, when "that which is godlike within us shall have joined with its like."[2] We have reviewed the various stages of this process as it appears in Gregory's soteriology. We must now, in a final chapter, briefly describe Gregory's concept of the heavenly state and then, with greater precision than has yet been possible, attempt a definition of what Gregory means by his oft-repeated assertion that one's final destiny is θεὸς γενέσθαι.

---

1. 2.2.4.83-3 (PG 37.1512).
2. Or. 27.17 (PG 36.48C) and above, pp. 32-6.

CHAPTER VIII -- THEŌSIS

The yearning for peace, quiet, and solitude which marked all of Gregory's life was in fact a yearning for an earthly approximation of that kind of life which he believed to characterize the heavenly state. But this desire to escape the world was, however, less of a dissatisfaction with the world than it was an eager anticipation for what lay ahead, namely, a joyful existence with Christ in the Jersualem above. Accordingly, when Gregory describes the heavenly state, it is often by means of a comparison to the instability and transitoriness of earthly existence. Heaven, for Gregory, is the end of a long and arduous journey, a peaceful haven sheltered from the storm-tossed waves of mortal life, a welcome rest for the Christian sojourner, and a final release from the vicissitudes of life.[1] Entrance into the new life of the kingdom is accompanied by that third and final "earthquake" which, at Christ's coming in judgment, transforms and changes the created order into a condition of unshakable stability.[2] The "storm of life" is turned into tranquility, anxiety into peace, darkness into light, and the constant yearning for knowledge of and presence with God into fulfillment. By rising from the limits of earthly life, the boundaries of "time" and "motion" are transcended.[3]

Yet Gregory's concept of the future life is not

---

1. Or. 18.3, 42 (PG 35.988D-999A, 1041B), etc. We can here give only a brief outline of Gregory's views on this and related subjects; for a fuller treatment, see J. Mossay, La mort et l'au-delà dans saint Grégoire de Nazianze (Louvain, 1966), as well as his "Perspectives eschatologiques de saint Grégoire de Nazianze," QLP, 4 (1964), pp. 320-39.

2. Or. 21.25 (PG 35.1109D), Or. 31.25 (PG 36.160D-161A).

3. Or. 39.8 (PG 36.341D).

solely one of negative contrast with the life of the present. His longing to reach the long sought-after goal is not informed only by a desire to have the journey done. He does, indeed, speak of death, the portal between this life and the next, as the cessation of evils;[1] life in the world he speaks of as the flight of a passing bird, as the passage of a ship leaving no trace of its presence on the sea's surface, or as a flower that quickly blooms and then even more quickly fades.[2] But death brings with it more than just a lowering of the tombstone, more than just a final return to dust.[3] The glory of the future life is found not so much in its being a termination of the Christian's journey through the world as in its being the creative fulfillment of that journey, the fruition of both its quality and its direction. Since, therefore, the heavenly state is the goal towards which the whole divine economy of creation, and then of re-creation, has been directed, it is perhaps better to describe one's attainment of this goal as the "beginning" of a new life rather than as the "end" of the old.

The images which Gregory employs to depict the quality of the new heavenly life are already familiar to us, especially the image of light. God is light, and those who approach God and become increasingly "godlike" are themselves then called light, because they reflect the first uncreated light.[4] To be in heaven, says Gregory, is to be filled with the light that streams from God; it is to be enlightened by the rays of Christ.[5] One enters the blessed state to be welcomed by the "unspeakable light" which is the vision of the glorious Trinity, and to circle, as a lesser light, the one great Light.[6]

Gregory has recourse to other New Testament meta-

---

1. Or. 7.20 (PG 35.780B).
2. Ibid., 19 (PG 35.777CD).
3. Ibid., 18 (PG 35.777B).
4. Or. 40.5 (PG 36.364C).
5. Or. 7.17 (PG 35.776C), Or. 8.19 (PG 35.812C).
6. Or. 16.9 (PG 35.945C), Or. 18.42 (PG 35.1041B).

phors when attempting to portray the nature of the life in the world to come. He speaks, for instance, of being in the "bosom of Abraham," of sharing the inheritance of Christ, of "reigning" with Christ, of being a "fellow-citizen" with Christ, and of partaking of the eternal feast and festival which will be the constant joy of those in heaven.[1] In the Jerusalem above, he goes on to say, we will enjoy to the full what we have tasted only as crumbs in this life, and will know at last that end to which the Scriptures point and to which the divine "mysteries" lead us.[2]

We see here in Gregory's language a recognizable conflation of two views, the biblical and the Platonic. The former uses specific texts, the large majority of them Pauline; the latter speaks of permanence and immobility, where even the "circling around" the one great Light represents perfection more of "form" than of "motion." Gregory in no way indicates that these two views are incompatible, but blends them together in such a way as to draw, as he sees it, upon the best from each of these two traditions.[3]

Permanence, illumination, nearness to God, knowledge of God, a joyful life with Christ--these are the marks of that future life for which Gregory himself longs and towards which he wishes to lead others. They constitute, for Gregory, the fulfillment of the very purposes for which God originally created us and for which, in the economy of salvation, he re-created us. They represent the "solid meat" which Adam in Paradise was unable to digest, the full mature "stature" into

---

1. Or. 7.17, 23 (PG 35.776C), Or. 8.6 (PG 35.796B), Or. 38.18 (PG 36.333A). By the "heavenly feast," Gregory apparently does not have in mind the "messianic banquet," since he goes on to define this "feast" as the contemplation of Christ's glory, a typically Gregorian concept, as we have already seen.

2. Or. 7.17 (PG 35.776C), Or. 8.23 (PG 35.816C).

3. To this extent, at least, Gregory's description of the heavenly life parallels his "theoretical" definition of Paradise in Or. 38.12 (PG 36.324B-D).

which Adam was created to grow, and the realization of that "yearning" for God with which Adam, by virtue of his being made in the image of God, was born.

If we recall Gregory's exposition of the steps by which God undertook, in the economy of the Body of Christ, to save mankind and direct it once more towards its created goal of theōsis, two further points emerge which are important to Gregory's understanding of the life to come. First of all, since it is the whole person that the Word assumed, and therefore the whole person that was saved, it will be the whole person, in all constituent parts, that will attain to the heavenly state. Death indeed is a separation of soul and body, but the dissolution of neither. When one dies, says Gregory, one's soul is "set free" from the "body" and, presumably in some intermediate state, awaits with a "sense" and "perception" of its future promise the time when it can go rejoicing to meet its Master. Then, a little later, the soul receives again its "kindred" flesh and, reunited, enters into the inheritance of glory, one in mind, one in spirit, and one with God.[1] Here again we see a conflation of scriptural and Platonic strains: the soul's joyful anticipation, after death, of final union with God reflects Gregory's hellenic background, while his insistence on the resurrection of the body indicates his dependence on the New Testament.[2]

_____

1. Or. 7.21 (PG 35.781C-784A). Since Gregory speaks thus of the soul's retention of sentient qualities after death, he appears to reject any view which would posit the "sleep" or "death" of the soul prior to its entrance into judgment.

2. For a brilliant discussion of the problems inherent in this issue, see H. A. Wolfson, "Immortality and Resurrection in the Philosophy of the Church Fathers," BHDS, 21 (1956-7), pp. 5-36, reprinted in Religious Philosophy: A Group of Essays (op. cit.), pp. 68-103. Gregory makes no mention, in this passage, of the concept that the martyr, upon death, goes directly to God without having to wait until the judgment and

From Gregory's assertion of a future "materiality" emerges a second point, namely, that, as the economy of the Holy Spirit provided for individual appropriation of the salvation made universally available in the
economy of the incarnation, so too we retain our individuality in the heavenly state. Because of the
body that rejoins the soul after death, it is necessarily distinguished from others as an individual. There
is no suggestion in Gregory of a future state where the
individual is so completely absorbed into the spiritual
cosmos that he is no longer himself. Because the whole
person is raised, his or her identity is retained in
heaven. If Gregory stresses the resurrection of the
body, he also gives assent to the Pauline assertion that
our heavenly flesh is not to be understood in an earthly manner; but flesh it is. There will be, however, in
the future life, no distinction between "male and female, barbarian, Scythian, bond or free, for such are
the marks of the flesh."[1] Gregory gives no indication
of the extent to which he believes the difference between male and female are to be obliterated in heaven;
he may just be using a text without being concerned
as to its literal meaning. To the androgynous state
of the mystery religions or to the concept of universal
maleness espoused by some gnostics, Gregory pays no
attention.[2] He does say, however, that sexual differ-
ences apply only to the body, and not to the soul, so
we would not be surprised were he to allow of some retention of sexual characteristics in heaven in as much
as the flesh one takes into heaven is not so spiritual

general resurrection; nor does he speak of the martyr
as sitting in judgment, with Christ, over those who put
him to death. Once Gregory does refer to the repentant
thief who was crucified with Jesus, but says only that
Jesus "saved" him, making no mention of an immediate
entry into Paradise; Or. 29.20 (PG 36.101B), Lk. 22.43.
    1. Or. 7.23 (PG 35.785C), Or. 30.6 (PG 36.112B).
    2. See, for instance, Hippolytus, Phil., 5.8; Gos-
pel of Thomas, Log. 114; Passio Sanct. Perpet. et
Felic., 10. For a survey of the literature on this

as to be indistinguishable from the angels who are, as
we have seen, immaterial and therefore presumably sex-
less. The continuing individuality of persons is based,
however, not only on the resurrection of the whole person, but also on the fact that each person entering
heaven is assigned a specific "mansion." Each of these
"many mansions in my Father's house" reflects the degree of virtue and purity achieved on earth by those
who will inhabit it.[1] In sum, individuality is not
obliterated in the future life any more than is our
whole psychosomatic constitution. Or, as Henry Chadwick
has put it--albeit in a non-Gregorian context--" Salvation means the annihilation not of individuality but
of the gulf between the finite and the infinite."[2] For
Gregory, since the "image" has been saved, and the flesh
"immortalized," the citizens of heaven will be recognized only by the divine "impress," by the image of God
by whom and for union with whom they were made.[3]

We can discover in Gregory's view of the final
state, then, a portrait the major elements of which
have a direct relation to his understanding of the

subject, see D. S. Bailey, Sexual Relations in Christian Thought (New York, 1959). As to sexual life on
earth, Gregory is a staunch advocate of virginity and
celibacy, but at the same time accepts of the goodness
of the married state if entered into in good faith
and if the wife, in her relation to her husband, has
Christ as her head, and can look forward to that day
when she will be the bride of Christ. See Or. 8.14, 19
(PG 35.805BC), Or. 37.10 (PG 36.293B-296A), Or.
40.08 (PG 36.381A-384A), Szymusiak, op. cit., pp. 60-5,
and Bouyer, op. cit., pp. 416-8.
     1. Or. 14.5 (PG 35.864B), Or. 30.4 (PG 36.108C),
and Or. 45.11 (PG 36.637BC). Lossky has interpreted
these "many mansions" from Jn. 14:2 to mean that in
the heavenly state the vision and apprehension of God
will not be the same for every individual; The Vision
of God (London, 1963), p. 36f.
     2. Chadwick, op. cit., p. 92.
     3. Or. 7.23 (PG 35.785C), Or. 38.13 (PG 36.325C).

economies of creation and salvation. Here, as elsewhere, Gregory fails to give us specific details as
to the manner in which these "last things" will come to
pass, and he thus leaves the modern interpreter with
many unanswered questions. He draws on many diverse
sources to construct his portrait of that life for
which he has yearned for so long, but remains at the
same time faithful to the spirit, if not the letter,
of the New Testament. But the one major principle which
informs his view of the heavenly state is that the divine purpose in creation is identical with the purpose
of salvation, namely that we were created, and then
recreated, to know and be with our Creator. Such knowledge of, and proximity to, God are the principle hall-
marks of the goal and end of this life, and thus of the
beginning of the next. We were created in the image of
God with the vocation of growing more and more into a
true and mature reflection of the Archetype.[1] The vision of God, long yearned for in this life, becomes,
in the future life, a reality when the image ascends
to its original and man becomes "godlike." Or, as G.
Ladner has pointed out, the recovery of the "image"
constitutes our "deification."[2] It is by virtue of
this image implanted in us that we have a "kinship"
with God; by virtue of this image, heaven, which is
God's abode, is also our true home; and it is by
virtue of this image that our natural desire for God

---

1. Theōsis, as a "reflection" of the Archetype, however, is not merely a noetic phenomenon, even though
the image, for Gregory, is located in the nous. As
Gross (op. cit., p. 245) has shown, because of the
"image," there is a parenté between the human mind and
the divine, but not a consubstantialité. We would question Holl's statement (op. cit., p. 166) that the chief
characteristic of man's progress towards "deification"
consists of his becoming nous, since God, by definition, is Nous. As we shall see infra, this is severely
to limit the concept of theōsis.
2. G. Ladner, The Idea of Reform (Cambridge, Mass.,
1959), p. 106.

and natural inclination towards God, when fulfilled,
becomes the definition of who we were created to be.[1]
   The future life, therefore, is a life in which
those who are saved become what God originally intended
them to be, namely, θεοί.[2] In our final state, says Gregory, "we shall be entirely godlike, able to receive
into ourselves the whole God and him alone, and this is
that perfection to which we press on."[3] After the final
judgment, says Gregory again, "God will stand in the
midst of gods, namely, those who have been saved."[4]
Theōsis, then, is the goal towards which the whole
ministry of Gregory, indeed the whole of creation, is
directed. Each and every creature of God is called θεός
εἶναι.[5] There is no part of Gregory's writings, whether
theological, christological or soteriological, whether
contemplative, pastoral or ascetical, in which this constant concern for theōsis is not a major motif, a motif
by which we today are the more able faithfully to interpret his thought. As was mentioned in an earlier part
of this study, theōsis is not a concept which strikes
Western ears with familiarity; to many it is a foreign,
and therefore unwelcome, term. It is for this reason
that the following concluding pages will be devoted to
an interpretation of theōsis, both to what it is as well
as to what it is not, as it appears in the thought of
the Nazianzen.

---

   1. It is in fact the image, says Gregory in one of
his poems, that "deifies"; 1.2.2.560-1 (PG 37.622).
See also Or. 2.22 (PG 35.432B), Or. 28.17 (PG 36.48C),
Or. 38.11-12 (PG 36.324A-C), Plagnieux, op. cit., pp.
20-7, 267, and Pinault, op. cit., p. 143. Szymusiak
(op. cit., p. 31) has rightly said that, for Gregory,
"l'image est la définition même de l'homme."
   2. See Or. 30.4 (PG 36.108C), an allusion to Ps.
81:1 (LXX).
   3. Or. 30.6 (PG 36.112B). This passage is omitted
from the NPNF translation but included in the LCC.
   4. Or. 30.4 (PG 36.108C).
   5. Or. 43.48 (PG 36.560A).

CONCLUSION

We have come now to the end of our survey of Gregory's understanding of the divine oikonomia in general and of his doctrine of salvation in particular. It would be easy to conclude with the brief assertion that, for Gregory, salvation and theōsis were interchangeable terms, yet, for all the indications that this is so, to make so facile an interpretation would be to oversimplify the terms themselves as well as to do an injustice to the thought of Gregory. Drawing several as yet unconnected threads together, therefore, we shall attempt to demonstrate that theōsis, while not the same as salvation, is certainly the one concept which we can employ as a primary interpretative tool in our endeavor to comprehend what salvation means. In so doing, it will become apparent that Gregory has made a unique contribution to the theological and soteriological thought of his and succeeding generations, our own included.

We would point out, first of all, that no Christian theologian prior to Gregory employed the term theōsis (or the idea contained in the term) with as much consistency and frequency as did he; both terminologically and conceptually Gregory went far beyond his predecessors in his sustained application of theōsis. Theophilus of Antioch was the first to use the vocabulary of theōsis but restricted its meaning to that of immortality.[1] Irenaeus was the first to relate the incarnation of the Word to the deification of man, postulating a "double metathesis" whereby God became man that man might become God.[2] Clement of Alexandria was the first to use the word θεοποιέω to indicate this "deifying" action brought about by the incarnation, re-

---

1. Ad Autol, 2.27.
2. Adv. haer., 3.19.1.

179

lating it to the contemporary hellenic concept of
"assimilation to God."[1] With Origen, "deification"
became established as a fully developed category of
Christian theology, but the difficulties inherent in
Origen's "system" tended to detract from the ultimate
validity of the term.[2] Perhaps the best-known pre-Gre-
gorian "deification" text is from Athanasius:[3]

αὐτὸς γὰρ ἐνηνθρώπησεν, ἵνα ἡμεῖς θεοποιηθῶμεν.

But not until Gregory, who must have known of these
prior attempts to give voice to this as yet hesitating-
ly formulated concept, do we find theōsis as no longer
an incidental or occasional motif in theological writings. Gregory himself was well aware that the constant
use he made of the doctrine of "deification," in numer-
ous contexts, must have been somewhat startling to his
congregation, recognizing, perhaps, that the terminology
he was using had not yet become firmly rooted in the
Christian tradition. This can be assumed from his fre-
quent recourse, when speaking of theōsis, to such phrases as:[4]

Θαρρῶ λέγειν.
εἰ μὴ τολμηρὸν τοῦτο εἰπεῖν.

Gross has suggested that Gregory employed such paren-
thetical insertions in order to soften the hardiesse
of his assertions.[5] On one occasion, Gregory even
said that there were some who "laughed at him" when

---

1. Paed., 1.12. On this subject, see H. Merki,
ὁμοίωσις Θεῷ . Von der Platonischen Angleichung an
Gott zur Göttahnlichkeit bei Gregor von Nyssa (Freiburg,
1952).
2. In Jo., 2.2 See H. Crouzel, Théologie de l'image
de Dieu chez Origène (Paris, 1956), pp. 164ff.
3. De inc., 54; also Contra Arianos, 3.25.
4. As in Or. 18.4 (PG 35.989B), Or. 45.13 (PG 36.
641A), etc. See Pinault, op. cit., p. 199.
5. Gross, op. cit., p. 249. Gross' study, the only

180

he described our divine origin and destiny in terms
of "deification."[1] But for all his recognition of the
"rashness" of his language, Gregory never held back,
and, as we have seen, applied the concept of "deification" to all aspects of the Christian faith. Perhaps he
realized, in the words of Georges Florovsky, that although theōsis "may be a hard word, it is the only
adequate phrase to express what is meant ."[2]

But, given the importance obviously assigned to
this concept, we must point out that he never once
sought to support it on scriptural grounds. Like homoousion, theōsis found its way into the Christian vocabulary from extra-biblical sources. But, as we can de-
duce from his explanation of the "novel" doctrine of
the deity of the Holy Spirit, this was no embarrassment
to Gregory since the validity of a specific doctrinal
term was based on its faithfulness to biblical ideas,
not to biblical words. Philological genealogies or
scriptural proof-texts did not determine, for Gregory,
the "orthodoxy" of a particular dogma or doctrine.[3]

---

of its kind, is a thorough and systematic survey of the
concept of "deification" in patristic literature. See
also his "Die Vergöttlichung des Christen nach den
griechischen Vätern," ZAM, 14 (1939), pp. 79-94. I
find it odd that in each of these studies Gross rele-
gates Gregory to that select group in whose writings
only "occasional" references to the doctrine of "deification" can be found. And A. Theodorou, in a more
recent study, hardly mentions Gregory at all: Ἡ περὶ
θεώσεωſ τοῦ ἀνθρώπου διδασκαλία (Athens, 1956). So
too with P. B. T. Bilaniuk's "The Mystery of Theōsis
or Divinization," in Nieman and Schatkin (eds.), The
Heritage of the Early Church (Rome, 1973), pp. 337ff.
   1. Or. 2.7 (PG 35.416A).
   2. Florovsky, "Lamb of God," p. 19.
   3. For some enthusiastic attempts to make of theōsis a scriptural term, as differentiated from a scriptural concept, see Ermoni, op. cit., pp. 509ff, and A.
Theodorou, "Die Lehre von der Vergottung des Menschen,"
KD, 7 (1961), pp. 285ff.

In spite of several attempts on the part of modern interpreters to derive theōsis from scripture, it would
be more accurate to say, with O. Faller, that theōsis
was common, before Gregory, to the Christian tradition,
but in "forms" that had no terminological parallels; it
reflected biblical "concepts," not biblical "texts."[1]
Or, as Plagnieux has said, "the absence of a word from
scripture in no way excludes . . . the presence of a
corresponding doctrine; . . . innovation of expression
does not imply an innovation of basics."[2]

   If Gregory's use of theōsis has but few Christian
parallels in earlier thought, and no terminological
relation to the vocabulary of scripture, must we then
turn to non-Christian parallels if we are to understand
what Gregory meant by it? R. Franks, for instance,
traces the concept of theōsis back through neo-platon-
ism to Plato, thence to Dionysios and primitive Orphism,
concluding that, because of such questionable ancestry,
"deification" cannot be considered a viable category
of Christian thought.[3] Yet, if we turn to the works of
Gregory himself, we will find ample evidence for an
opposite conclusion, namely, that Gregory was quite
aware of the "pagan" parallels to theōsis; more than
this, he quite consistently repudiated the various
expressions of "deification" as found in his non-Christian inheritance. Of the many occurrences of "deification" in pre- and non-Christian literature, we can
point to four of which Gregory was aware and which he
criticized as not being consonant with the idea of

---

   1. O. Faller, "Griechischen Vergottung und christliche Vergöttlichung," Greg, 6 (1925), p. 241.
   2. Plagnieux, op. cit., p. 61. G. Butterworth has
suggested that "deification" was a terminological im-
possibility given the Jewish monotheistic background
of Christianity: "The Deification of Man in Clement
of Alexandria," JTS, 17 (1916), p. 163. See also Gross,
op. cit., p. 347.
   3. R. Franks, "The Idea of Salvation in the Theology
of the Eastern Church," Mansfield College Essays (London, 1909), pp. 249-64.

"deification" as he used it within the corpus of his
own writings.

(1) It might be possible, for one approach, to accuse Gregory of outright idolatry in his articulation
of the concept of theōsis. Does not the "deification of
man" suggest that the honor and praise due the Creator
has been transferred to the creature? Yet we have seen
that Gregory was quite specific in his condemnation
of any such idea. In his discussion of the fall, he
pointed to that Adamic pride which sought to substitute
himself for God, a pride which arose out of his exalted state and was evil prey for the Devil's envy. Sin
entered the created universe when Lucifer sought to be
"thought of as God" and we, in our turn, reached out
impatiently for the destiny that was to be ours, but
not yet.[1] Which is to say, between the jealous "desire"
to be God and God's creative purposes for the final
human destiny, there can be, and was for Gregory, no
similarity at all. Gregory even asserted, as we saw,
that idolatry, i.e., the worship of anything less than
God, was the major mark of our fallen state, of our
separation from God, and of our divergence from that
path which led to our ultimate "deification." The vocabulary of "deification," then, was used by Gregory
precisely to expose the danger of confusing theōsis
with idolatry. Time and again Gregory inveighed against
those who "deified" any created object, whether celestial bodies, visible things, or even--with Paul, the
belly![2] So Gregory knew what idolatry meant; but in
his concept of theōsis we can find no trace of any
failure to render to the Creator sole honor and praise.

(2) Similarly, given Gregory's vocabulary, the historian might be tempted to associate the concept of
theōsis with the many and varied beliefs and practises
of the Greek mystery religions. Yet we find that Gregory was surprisingly well-informed as to these mys-

---

1. Or. 36.5 (PG 36.269CD).
2. Or. 28.13-15 (PG 36.44B-45A), Or. 40.39 (PG 36.
416A).

183

teries and was familiar with their major tenets, whether
magical, astrological, or sacrificial. Yet he dismissed
them all as pure "nonsense," as the dark invention of
demons, as myths and fables wanting in reason.[1] Although
he made no specific mention of their "deificatory" rites,
he did take the opportunity to ridicule those Greeks who
deemed as "gods" those who "reek of sacrifices."[2] And in
his Oration on the Holy Lights, he showed little restraint in his bitter attack on the various mystery religions, their vile practises and foolish beliefs, concluding that they are good for nothing but the amuse-
ment of the children of the Greeks and the demons.[3]

(3) In like manner Gregory dismissed as ridiculous
what today remains as the most familiar form of "deification," namely, imperial apotheōsis, the idea that the
Emperor, upon death, was transformed into a god. Gregory's profound scorn for such a view is perhaps best
seen in his Second Invective against Julian. Exploiting
a current, but most probably spurious, tale, Gregory
told of how the Emperor, when mortally wounded in his
battle against the Persians, recalled that some of his
predecessors had aimed at being higher than mortals and
had contrived to disappear and thereby get themselves
"accounted as gods." With this in mind, Gregory went
on to say, Julian tried throwing himself in the river,
hoping that if his body were never discovered he too
would be acclaimed as a "new god," or, at least (Gregory commented) by those who were stupid enough to
be taken in by such a deception. Fortunately an imperial eunuch discovered Julian in the process of entering the water, and the deception failed.

But if Gregory could thus ridicule the cultic "dei-

---

1. Or. 39.3 (PG 36.336C-337A).
2. Or. 38.6 (PG 36.316D).
3. Or. 39.5-7 (PG 36.340A-341C).
4. Or. 5.14 (PG 35.681AB). Julian was not, however,
without friends to champion his apotheōsis. Libanius,
for instance, speaks of temples built to Julian in
which he was worshipped as a god, where prayers were
offered up to him, and where blessings have been forth-

184

fication" of those who wear the purple, at the same time
he could speak of another "deification" where rulers are
concerned. Addressing his words to basileis in general,
he wrote: "That which is above belongs to the one God;
that which is below belongs to you. Become, if I may
use a bold expression, gods to those who are under your
rule." That is, exercise your power with charity and
wisdom, imitating the philanthrōpia of God. Thus, the
deificatory role of mimēsis, which we discussed earlier,
could be applied to all people by Gregory, even to those
who wore the purple, but never in the sense of traditional apotheōsis.

(4) A final possible interpretation which we might
give of Gregory's concept of theōsis, if we refer to
its non-Christian parallels, is to conclude that it too
easily lends itself, if not to outright idolatry, at
least to polytheism on the one hand, or pantheism on
the other. But, again, nowhere in Gregory's writings
do we find any expression of either a plurality of gods

---

coming from the deceased Emperor. So, obviously, comments Libanius, Julian "has ascended to heaven and has
partaken of the power of the divine by the will of the
gods themselves." Or. 18.304 (see also Or. 24, Upon
Avenging Julian). The literature on the subject of imperial "deification" is vast; among the more important
titles are A. D. Nock, "Deification and Julian," JRS,
47 (1957), pp. 115-23; E. Lohmeyer, Christuskult und
Kaiserkult (Tübingen, 1919); A. Strong, Apotheosis and
After Life (London, 1915); E. Cumont, After Life in
Roman Paganism (New Haven, 1922). For further titles,
consult the bibliography appended to E. R. Bevan, "Deification (Greek and Roman)," in J. Hastings (ed.),
Encyclopedia of Religion and Ethics, Vol. 4 (New York,
1922), pp. 525-33.

1. Or. 36.11 (PG 36.277C). On the hellenic concept
of kingship and the related issue of deification, to
which Gregory here gives voice, see F. Dvornik, Early
Christian and Byzantine Political Philosophy--Origins
and Background, Dumbarton Oaks Studies, 9 (Locust Val-
ley, N.Y., 1966), pp. 207-25, 492-500, and passim.

or an identification of the created world with the
Creator. The abyss, in a word, that separates the
"deified" person from the "deifying" God is never
bridged. G. L. Prestige has said this well in a reference to the patristic tradition of deification:
" Such expressions of the deification of man, are, it
must be remembered, purely relative. . . The Fathers
explained the lower in terms of the higher, but did not
obliterate the distinction between them. . .[M]ankind
in general can only aspire to that sort of divinity
which lies open to its capacity through union with the
divine humanity."[1] In Gregory's case, a creature was a
creature, and would always remain so, even after the
attainment of theōsis. No one can ever threaten the
unique status of the Godhead numerically (polytheism)
or substantially (pantheism). Our created vocation of
progressing towards theōsis does not do away with our
creatureliness; rather, it fulfills it. For one to be
"deified" is to be a "creature" of God, as God intended
one to be. Theōsis, as Gregory once said, cannot be
taken "literally"; one cannot literally "become God"
since that would be as absurd as if we were to state
that God is a "creature." If God is a creature, then
he is, by definition, not God, for only creatures
have a beginning in time. Only God is "uncreated";
the creature, therefore, is just that, a creature,
and οὐ θεόſ.[2] Or, as Brooks Otis has expressed it even
more precisely, the "deification" of man was, for Gre-

---

1. G. L. Prestige, God in Patristic Thought (London, 1952), pp. 74f.
2. Or. 42.17 (PG 36.477C). M. F. Wiles has underlined this point in reference to the Fathers: When
they spoke in terms of "divinization," i.e., of God
becoming what we are in order that we might become
what he is, "they did not intend the parallelism to
be taken with full seriousness. . . In speaking of
man's divinization the Fathers intended to convey
that men should become gods only in a secondary sense--
'gods by grace.' . . It was never believed that they
would become what the Word was, 'God by nature.'"

gory, a concept which at once depicted God as "unap-
proachably remote from, and inseparably close to, man."[1]
Gregory in no way identified God with the world, therefore, or with any part of it, including mankind; nor the
world with God.[2] As intimately related as God always
has been to his creation through the divine oikonomia,
he is always "above" and distinct from it. Theōsis does
not eliminate this distinction.

There are many things, then, that theōsis is not.
Until the time of Gregory, it was not a central category of Christian thought. Nor is theōsis a concept
which admits of scriptural proof-texting. And finally,
theōsis is not a term which can be interpreted through
sole recourse to its non-Christian parallels, whether
idolatry, cultic imperial apotheōsis, polytheism, or
pantheism. Gregory did not ignore this non-Christian
background; he explicitly refuted it.

But to describe theōsis in terms of what it is
not, while helpful in protecting us from the dangers
of an overly facile or prejudiced interpretation, does
not yet give us a positive concept of what it is. How
can we describe it in such a way so as to be faithful
both to the thought of Gregory as well as to the in-
tegrity of traditional Christian faith? Is is possible,
in fact, to reach back into the fourth century and
rescue a term that is all but forgotten in the modern
theological enterprise?

Perhaps the first thing we can say is that, for
Gregory, theōsis was descriptive of a relation between
God and creation not a definition either of us or of
God separate from one another. Although we and God are
separated as creature and Creator, the gulf in
between is not absolute, the distance not infinite.
From the time of creation, mankind and the Creator
have been bound together, first by God's creative

The Making of Christian Doctrine (Cambridge, 1969),
pp. 107ff.

1. B. Otis, "The Throne and the Mountain," p. 163.
2. See Lot-Borodine, op. cit., 107, p. 47, and O.
Faller, op. cit., p. 427.

goodness which called us into being, and subsequently by the divine oikonomia which has ever sought to guide us towards our ordained destiny. The only unbridgeable gap between us and God is of our own making; only we, by free choice, can turn our backs on God, for God will never turn his back on creation. The "infinity" of God can be described, then, not in terms of the distance between God and us, but in terms of the conviction that no matter how far we flee from our Creator, we are never beyond the infinite reach of God's creative and redeeming compassion. This abiding relation between God and humankind is also part of our created nature. Our somatic constitution, as we have seen, is "akin" to our noetic and spiritual nature; and our spiritual nature, by virtue of the "image of God" breathed into us by the Creator Word, is, in turn, "akin" to God.[1]

If theōsis, then, expresses a relation between us and God, a second thing we must say is that this relation can in no way be described as "static." We were created to grow into an increasingly intimate relation with God. Therefore, theōsis is a term which must be described dynamically, for the potential for growth is infinite, yet at no one time can it be said to be fully achieved.[2]

It must further be noted that theōsis, as a "dynamic" term descriptive of the divine-human "relation," in the long run says more of God than it does of us. This is because the initiative for the relationship, as well as the ability to grow dynamically in it, depends on God. The process of theōsis, then, is adoptive, not natural. It is "natural," said Gregory, for man to become God, but by this he meant that it was in accordance with the divine plan, and that the "initiated"

---

1. Or. 7.21 (PG 35.213B), Or. 14.8 (PG 35.868A).
2. R. Franks, on the other hand, states (The Work of Christ, p. 100) that only with Augustine did the Greek idea of "deification" lose its "natural" and "physical" dimensions and come to be described in "ethical" and "adoptive" categories.

man who knows both his origin and his destiny knows that they are divine.[1] The "deity" of the Persons of the Trinity, Gregory constantly asserted to be φύσει οὐ θέσει . But he also insisted that the divine status of the "deified" man is adoptive (θετόſ).[2]

Thus far, in summary, we can say that, for Gregory, theōsis was a term by which he sought to indicate a dynamic relation between God and mankind, a relationship which is dependent upon God's creative and sustaining initiative, resulting in our progressive growth towards an adopted dignity of fulfilled creatureliness. To this extent, then, we can say that our "deification" is analogous to the "deification" of Christ's human nature, but not identical. The union effected within the one Person of Christ, as we have seen, was effected by the "presence" of the divine nature; the divine "deified," and the human was "deified."[3] Thus, for Gregory, the "deification" of Christ's human nature became the principle upon which our analogous "deification" is based. But, within the economy of salvation, theōsis is not limited to the incarnation event. Rather, Gregory saw theōsis as a process having its initial roots in the purposes of creation, a purpose recreated in the incarnate life and death of Christ, perfected in the economy of the Holy Spirit, appropriated individually in baptism, as well as in ascetic and philanthropic imitation, and finally realized in the future life.[4] Accordingly, for Gregory, there could be no one point in time, past, present, or future, at which "deification" could be said to have taken place.

---

1. 1.2.33.222-3 (PG 37.144), Or. 8.6 (PG 35.796B). See also Szymusiak, op. cit., p. 73, no. 23.
2. 1.2.10.141-2 (PG 37.690), 2.2.5.45 (PG 37.1524).
3. Or. 38.13 (PG 36.325B), Ep. 101 (PG 37.180A).
4. Here again is evidence that salvation cannot, for Gregory, be said to have been effected by the "event" of the incarnation. Nor does the evidence Gregory gives us support the thesis that the Greek concept of "deification" sprang from the attempt to understand the delay of the parousia and was in fact

Because theōsis is a process and not an event, Gregory's understanding of the growth towards our ultimate destiny as neither violent, instantaneous, nor mechanical must be kept in mind. Both the definition of who we are, as well as the description of our pilgrimage towards fulfillment, depend on this concept of growth. Just as there is no one "time" within the divine economy which can be called specifically "deificatory," so too we can point to no one act of God or of man, to no one single sacrament or human virtue, as that by means of which theōsis is effected. Everything, at least potentially, contributes to our deification. The vast succession of divine acts are the means by which we can once more continue to grow into the divinely intended "creature" God calls us to be, but no one of these acts, by itself, is the one to which we can point and say, "Now we have been saved." So, too, the vast gamut of human responses to these divine acts all contribute to the salvific process. By reason of our created capacity for free choice, we can ourselves play a direct role in our own salvation; indeed we must. But, as we have seen, the constant potential for growth never eliminates the continuing potential for decay. In spite of God's eternal salvific concern and activity, we can be the source of our own undoing.

There is yet another point which must be made before we attempt our final analysis of Gregory's concept of theōsis. When Gregory spoke of the "growth" towards mankind's created goal, there is every indication that he conceived of this growth as having a double direction only, that is, "forward," or, to use the more common metaphor, "upwards." But after the fall there appears to be, in Gregory's understanding of it, both a "backwards" movement to the previously unfallen

---

little else than a complete abandonment of Pauline orthodoxy for an uneschatologically oriented hellenism; see M. Werner, Die Entstehung des christlichen Dogmas, 2nd ed. (Tübingen, 1941), pp. 389-420.

state as well as a "forward" movement towards the originally intended state of fulfillment. The salvation
achieved by the Son of God takes us back to our original creation, placing us, as it were, once more on
the road from which we had diverged. But this salvation
also takes us forward and places us further along
on that road. To this extent, then, salvation is the
"recovery," a means of "returning" to Adam's first condition.[1] Yet we have seen that Gregory did not think of
Paradise as a state of perfection or fulfillment. Adam,
as created, was immature; he was created to grow. Therefore, in opposition to the Origenistic view that a recovery of the unfallen state is all that is necessary,
Gregory adopted the Irenaean view that salvation also
places us on a higher level than the one we had at-
tained before we fell. It is for this reason that Gregory could speak of salvation, or re-creation, as being
a more exalted and godlike creation than the first.[2]
Salvation is not just a return to a primordial good.
If it were, the concept of theōsis would be meaningless. Rather, it is a return to a previous "capacity"
for growth so that the advance towards theōsis might
once more be undertaken. Here again we see the need
for approaching salvation more as a dynamic "process"
rather than as a static condition.

Because of this double direction which we find in
Gregory's description of the salvific process, it
would be unwise to define theōsis solely by reference
to one's final destiny. What theōsis means for the
redeemed person in the heavenly state applies also
at any stage of the progress towards ultimate fulfillment. The past, present, and future, therefore,
inform each other, lending to Gregory's understanding

---

1. Or. 38.4, 16-17 (PG 36.316A, 329C-332A).
2. Or. 40.7 (PG 36.365C). We cannot interpret Gregory's thought here as indicating that a "redeemed"
universe has more intrinsic value than one that never
needed to be redeemed since, in the Gregorian scheme,
even had man not fallen, the world as created was
still short of perfection.

of theōsis a more fluid quality than has generally been recognized. T. Sinko, for instance, has written that "Θεὸς γενέσθαι est finis vitae Christianae apud Gregorianum."[1] One cannot claim such a statement to be wrong; it is however limited in as much as theōsis is best understood as a reference, not only to the end but to the beginning as well, including everything in between. M. Lot-Borodine is therefore more accurate in her description of "déification" as anticipated and begun in via and fully realized in patria.[2] It need not surprise us, then, when we find Gregory speaking of theōsis as both a future goal and a present attainment. It is effected "here below"; it is also conferred in the "future life."[3] Or, as Gregory expressed it elsewhere, in this life (ἐνταῦθα) we are trained for our destiny and then are placed elsewhere (ἀλλαχοῦ), "deified" by our inclination towards God.[4]

Our attempt to arrive at a full appreciation of what Gregory intended by his constant use of the term theōsis (and its cognates) must therefore take into account both the fluidity of the term as well as its breadth. Theōsis is descriptive of a relation, but a relation that is constantly changing and multi-directional. It is descriptive also of a human condition, but a condition that defies temporal limitations.

---

1. T. Sinko, De traditione, p. 113, n. 3. Cf. Holl, op. cit., p. 166.

2. Lot-Borodine, op. cit., p. 21. See also her "Initiation à la mystique sacramentaire de l'Orient," RSPT, 24 (1935), p. 665. Szymusiak (op. cit., p. 76) expresses the same balanced approach in his statement that theōsis is "ébauchée sur la terre, rendue parfait dans l'au delà." Inge (op. cit., pp. 367ff) is even more elaborate: " Deification is a progressive transformation after the pattern revealed in Christ; a process which has as its end real union with God, though this end is, from the nature of things, unrealizable in time."

3. Or. 21.2 (PG 35.1084C).

4. Or. 38.11 (PG 36.324A).

There is no "now" to Gregory's concept of theōsis since, as a process of growth, it is initiated in the past, perfected in the future, and shaped in the present both by the past and the future. For this reason, theōsis cannot be defined as the exact equivalent of salvation. The former has its roots in the creative past, the latter in the re-creative past. Only as the purposes of both creation and re-creation are similar can theōsis and salvation be thought of as identical. More precisely, salvation is the "stronger medicine" applied to the "crooked sapling" so that the originally planted seed may grow in the direction in which it was intended to grow, namely, towards God.

Theōsis, accordingly, because of the variety of contexts in which Gregory saw fit to apply the terms, escapes strict definition. To define a concept at all too often restricts the concept to the limits of the definition. Theōsis, as a dynamically fluid term that is descriptive of the creative and salvific economy as well as of the relation between God and creation, will not suffer so to be limited. Rather than a "definition," then, we will, as our conclusion, attempt a verbal "approach" to theōsis which will at once be faithful to Gregory and to our own theological concerns. In this "approach" to theōsis, we recognize, as a methodological base, that "deification," both as a word and as a concept, is, like most theological language, a metaphor. It is, in a word, the verbal modality by which the distance between reality and our manifold attempts to describe reality is minimized, but never totally eliminated. Theōsis, as a metaphor, was used by Gregory on several levels of thought and in various arenas of concern, to express the reality which he felt to be coexistent with God's creative and redemptive purposes. Our approach to an understanding of this metaphor involves our comprehending theōsis in a six-fold dimension.

(1) Theōsis is first of all a spatial metaphor. In the conceptual framework of the fourth century where heaven was "up" and earth was "down," Gregory could speak of his progress towards his created and re-created destiny, not only as "growth," but also as

an "ascent" to his final resting place "close to
God."[1] In the economy of salvation, as we have seen,
this "ascent" was made possible only through the condescending "descent" of God in the Person of his Son.
As a relatively naive metaphor, Gregory's concept of
"ascent" and of our final "proximity" to God does
not allow of a metaphysical interpretation. There is
no idea in this metaphor of our being transformed
into God or absorbed into the divine being. When Gregory spoke of deification as an ascent to heaven so
that we might be close to God, he meant just that.[2]

(2) Theōsis, in the second place, can be understood as a visual metaphor. As such, it is descriptive
as of the "reflection" of God's brightness.[3] Because
of the deified person's proximity to God, the Sinaic
"cloud" no longer separates one from God; in the divine brightness there are no shadows, and vision is un-
impaired. God is light, and we were created to see God
as light and ourselves to reflect that light. The
popular reference to baptism as "illumination" in
patristic thought was but one use of this visual
metaphor to describe the process of theōsis.[4]

(3) We can understand theōsis also as an epistemological metaphor. An intrinsic part of our longing to

---

1. Or. 3.1 (PG 35.517A), Or. 11.5 (PG 35.837C), Or.
21.2 (PG 35.1084C), Or. 30.21 (PG 36.133A), etc.
2. Gross has seized upon this image of ascent (op.
cit., p. 348), seeing it as the complement of the divine ascent, and has said: "Déification obtenue par
l'initiation chrétienne doit être le point de départ
d'une ascension constante vers une divinisation tou-
jours plus parfaite." We would only add that, for Gregory, theōsis begins in creation, and not only with
baptism. Gross appears here to use, as do many French
authors, "divinisation" and "déification" as synonyms.
3. Or. 27.9 (PG 36.24A), Or. 40.5 (PG 36.364C),
412C), 1.2.1.210-4 (PG 37.538), etc.
4. Pinault's description (op. cit., p. 113) is
most apt: "L'homme est incapable de connaître entière-

see God is the desire to know God even as one is known. We have already seen that the philosophical life, for Gregory, was but one expression of this attempt to free himself of the "world" so that nothing would interfere with his advancing knowledge of the Triune Godhead. So too with his concept of the theological enterprise: we can never know God as he is in himself, only as he is for us, that is, "economically." And basic to our knowledge of God is the created "godlikeness" of those who, when joined to their like, become instruments of increasing awareness of who God is and of who they can be.[1]

It is unnecessary, of course, to underline the fact that the metaphors of "space," "vision," and "knowledge" are all different ways of saying the same thing. They all point to that element in us which, for Gregory, gives ample indication both of our divine origin and of our divine destiny. And in each case, the initiative is with God: only as God descends, can we ascend; only as God illumines, can we see; and only as God reveals, can we know. All three metaphors, no one of them unique to Gregory, are used to express his conviction that we were created to be with God, to behold our God, and to know him in his triune majesty.

(4) Another metaphor by means of which Gregory sought to express his understanding of theōsis we

---

ment la nature divine. Pourtant, voir et posséder Dieu, tel est son plus ardent désir. Veut-il l'atteindre, du moins, autant qu'on peut le rêver ici-bas? Veut-il préparer, ébaucher même la contemplation de l'au-delà? Qu'il se purifie, qu'il s'élève jusqu'à l'union déifiante, à la θέωσιϛ. Alors son esprit sera illuminé; son regard percevra Dieu. Telle est, dans les lignes essentielles, la méthode grégorienne d'ascension vers Dieu.

1. See Or. 28.17 (PG 36.48C). Ladner has suggested (op. cit., p. 98) that "deification" has this epistemological element because it is the continuation of the idea that "to know" is ultimately the same thing as "to be," and that "knowledge of God" therefore leads to "assimilation to God."

might best categorize as ethical. In the case of proximity, vision, and knowledge, the initiative is with
God. But because theōsis describes a relation, one must
oneself appropriate what has been given by God, i.e.,
the means of growing in closeness to, vision and knowledge of, God. For Gregory, this meant imitating the
very means by which God undertook to save us and to
restore us on the path towards theōsis, imitating,
that is, both the mode and the direction of God's salvific action, through ascetic endeavors on the one
hand, and philanthropic concern on the other. By so
doing, we participate in, and become co-agents of,
our own salvation, but always understood in a way that
sees grace and free will as both necessary to salvation,
and never playing them off against each other as one
might play Augustine off against Pelagius. Theōsis was
for Gregory both a gift and a reward, since by imitating, through the grace of God's creative gifts, the
mercy of God, one became more and more "godlike."[1]

(5) Theōsis is also a corporate metaphor indicating
the progressive "union" of the Christian with God. This
has always been a difficult concept to come to terms
with without indulging in mystical flights of fancy
and is therefore a concept which has been much criticized. One author, for instance, has seen in the idea,
common to Greek thought, of "union with God," often
expressed by the word "deification," the "more serious
aberration to be found not only in Origen but in the
whole tradition to which he contributed," a part of
which tradition, of course, was Gregory of Nazianzus.[2]
Modern defenders of the concept of "union with God"
have been accused, in fact, of perpetuating the doctrine of apotheōsis![3] But such suspicions are ill-
founded. Proximity to, vision and knowledge of God all
demand some sort of conceptual framework in which the

---

1. Or. 14.26-7 (PG 35.892C-893A), Or. 17.9 (PG 35.
976CD), Or. 36.11 (PG 36.277C), Ep. 178 (PG 37.293A).
2. So B. Drewery, Origen and the Doctrine of Grace
(London, 1960), p. 200.
3. Ibid. See also R. Greer's remark concerning

Christian's union with God can become a reality. To
speak of the former without at least attempting to
articulate the latter is nonsense. When Gregory spoke
of theōsis as the ultimate union between us and God,
he always maintained, as we have seen, the qualitative
distinction between creature and Creator. Yet he was so
convinced of the intended intimacy which was to exist
between us and God that he chose to describe this union
in "divine" rather than in "human" vocabulary.

(6) Finally, theōsis is a social metaphor. "Union
with God" could not, for Gregory, be limited to a static
participation, as the well-known Petrine text puts it,[1]
in the divine nature. Participation was also a dynamic
sharing of the divine life. Which is to say, it is not
enough merely to suggest that our destiny is to share
in those characteristics which are uniquely divine,
i.e., immortality and incorruptibility.[2] As Florovsky

"deification" in his Theodore of Mopsuestia: Exegete
and Theologian (London, 1961), pp. 14ff. Szymusiak, on
the other hand, quite approves of Gregory's idea of
theōsis as union with God: for Gregory, such union
(in this case, with Christ) is "tout le programme chrétien: posséder le Christ ou se laisser par lui, c'est
tout un." "Grégoire de Nazianze et le péché," SP, 9
(Texte und Untersuchungen, 94), p. 305.

1. 2 Pet. 1:4. Browne and Swallow (NPNF, 7, p. 228)
have commented that, for Gregory, theōsis is a "very
strong expression to bring out the reality and intimacy of the Christian's union with Christ as the result
of the sanctifying grace by which all the baptized are
made 'partakers of the Divine Nature.'" Yet, as we have
seen, Gregory does not use this text to support his
"corporate" understanding of theōsis; nor, of course,
does he limit his concept of "deification" to that
which is effected at baptism. Cf. also E. Mersch, Le
Corps Mystique du Christ, 3rd ed. (Paris, 1951), pp.
441ff and L. Bouyer, op. cit., pp. 418ff. For a helpful discussion of theōsis as "union," see V. Lossky,
The Mystical Theology of the Eastern Church, Ch. 10.

2. See G. Butterworth, op. cit., pp. 157ff, and the

has said, "Christians . . . aspire to something greater than natural immortality. They aspire to an everlasting communion with God. . . . Theōsis means no more than an intimate communion of human persons with the Living God. To be with God means to dwell in Him and to share His perfection."[1]

It would appear, therefore, that Gregory's consistent use of the concept of theōsis was an implicit acknowledgement of the limitations of human language to describe a divine reality. There were many metaphors available to him--six of which we have mentioned--whereby he could attempt a description of that reality which he saw as the underlying purpose of God's creative and redemptive activity. God created, and then saved, us for himself. Theōsis, accordingly, became the one "shorthand" metaphor under which all the other possible metaphors could be subsumed. And it was the more pertinent because its linguistic root was from the word "god," not "man." As bold an expression as it was in Gregory's day, and as startling as it may even seem now, in Gregory's hands it became the metaphor, along with its cognates (i.e., θεὸς γενέσθαι, θεοποιεῖν, θεοῦν), to express something that could ultimately be expressed only by God.

Theōsis, then, is not solely a soteriological term. Gregory's doctrine of salvation did indeed make ample use of the idea of "deification," both in its christological and anthropological dimensions.[2] Yet we must conclude that the constant reference to theōsis made by Gregory throughout his writings, be they on whatever

---

reply by C. Lattey, "The Deification of Man in Clement of Alexandria: Some Further Notes," JTS, 17 (1916), pp. 257ff.

1. Florovsky, "The Resurrection of Life," p. 26.
2. It would be possible, of course, to avoid the approach we have taken and relegate the meaning of "deification" to a functional role, that is, to see it only as an instrument used by the Greek Fathers to

subject or in whatever context, indicates that it is
more properly understood as a theological term. That
is, it helps us the better to know (1) who God is,
(2) what God has done for us, and therefore (3) who
we are and can be. The limits of human language to
which Gregory was subject, and to which we are subject, forced him to speak of God as a "man." By the
same token, given his vision of the destiny of creation,
he was compelled to speak of a creaturely human being
as a "god." Or, to put it more accurately, Gregory's
"doctrine" of the triune Godhead and of the whole
infinite span of God's activity - creative, redemptive,
and perfecting - on our behalf pointed consistently to
an abiding relation of intimacy between us and God.
For Gregory, this relation was so intimate, both in
its origin as well as in its future fulfillment, that
he could speak of it in two complementary ways. When
he sought to describe God's role in the relationship,
he spoke "anthropomorphically." In the same way, when
he attempted to describe what happens to us within
the dimensions of this relationship, i.e., theōsis,
he could well afford to speak "theomorphically."

---

bolster their already somewhat shaky arguments for the
divinity of the Son and/or the divinity of the Spirit.
It should be clear by now, however, that, were we to
do so, the whole theological enterprise in the East
from the 3rd to the 5th century would become immediately
suspect. We must ask critical questions of that enterprise, but questions which are precise enough to allow
us to separate the chaff from the wheat. Cf. M. Wiles,
"Soteriological Arguments," pp. 321ff.

BIBLIOGRAPHY

Primary Sources

Barbel, J. (ed.). Gregor von Nazianz: Die fünf theo-
    logischen Reden. Düsseldorf, 1963.

Billius, J. and Morellus, C. (ed.). Sancti Patris
    nostri Gregorii Nazianzeni Theologi. Opera.
    Paris, 1630 and 1690.

Boulanger, F. (ed.). Grégoire de Nazianze: Discours
    funèbres en l'honneur de son frère Césaire et de
    Basile de Césarée. Paris, 1908.

Browne, C. and Swallow, J. (eds.). Select Orations
    and Select Letters of Saint Gregory Nazianzen.
    ("A Select Library of Nicene and Post-Nicene
    Fathers," Second Series, Vol. 7.) Grand Rapids,
    1955.

Clemencet, P. and Caillau, D. (eds.). Sancti Patris
    nostri Gregorii Theologi, vulgo Nazianzeni, Arch-
    episcopi Constantinopolitani, Opera omnia quae
    extant. Paris, 1778-1842.

Deferrari, J. (ed.). Funeral Orations by Saint Gregory
    Nazianzen and Saint Ambrose. ("The Fathers of the
    Church," Vol. 22.) New York, 1953.

Devolder, E. (ed.). Saint Grégoire de Nazianze: Homé-
    lies. Namur (belg.), 1961.

_____. Saint Grégoire de Nazianze: Poèmes, Lettres,
    Discours. Namur (belg.), 1960.

Gallay, P. (ed.). Grégoire de Nazianze. Selections.
    Paris, 1959.

201

Gallay, P. (ed.). Saint Grégoire de Nazianze: Lettres
(2 vols). Paris, 1964 and 1967.

_____. Grégoire de Nazianze: Lettres Théologiques.
(Sources Chrétiennes, 208.) Paris, 1974.

Guillon, M. (ed.). Bibliothèque choisie des Pères
de l'Eglise greque et latine, Vols. 6 & 7.
Brussels, 1828.

Hardy, E. R. (ed.). The Christology of the Later
Fathers. ("Library of Christian Classics, 3.)
Philadelphia, 1954.

Hamman, A. (ed.). Le baptême d'après les pères de
l'Eglise. Paris, 1962. {Contains a translation
of Or. 40}

_____. Riches et pauvres dans l'Eglise ancienne.
Paris, 1962. {Contains a translation of Or. 15
and of select poems}

King, C. W. (ed.). Julian the Emperor. London, 1888.
{Contains Gregory's two Invectives against
Julian--Or. 4 & 5}

Mason, A. J. (ed.). The Five Theological Orations of
Gregory of Nazianzus. ("Cambridge Patristic
Texts.") Cambridge, 1899.

Migne, J. P. (ed.). Patrologia cursus completus,
series Graeca, Vol. 35-38. Paris, 1857-62.

Paton, W. R. (ed.). "The Epigrams of St. Gregory the
Theologian," in The Greek Anthology, Vol. 2.
("Loeb Classical Library.") New York, 1917.

Rufinus, Tyranius. Orationem Gregorii Nazianzeni
novem. (Corpus scriptorum ecclesiasticorum
latinorum, 56.) Leipzig, 1910.

Toal, M. E. (ed.). The Sunday Sermons of the Great
Fathers, Vol. 4. London, 1963. {Contains Or. 15}

Vérin, J. H. (ed.). Grégoire de Nazianze: Panégyrique des Macchabées. Paris, 1903.

Secondary Sources

Althaus, H. Die Heilslehre des heiligen Gregor von Nazianz. Münster, 1972.

Altaner, B. "Augustinus, Gregor von Nazianz und Gregor von Nyssa." Revue Bénédictine, 41 (1951).

Aubineau, M. "Incorruptibilité et divinisation selon Irénée." Recherches de science religieuse, 44 (1956).

Balas, D. L. ΜΕΤΟΥΣΙΑ ΘΕΟΥ. Man's Participation in God's Perfections according to Saint Gregory of Nyssa. (Studia Anselmia, 55.) Rome, 1966.

Balthasar, H. von. Présence et pensée. Paris, 1942.

Barmann, B. C. A Christian Debate of the Fourth Century: A Critique of Classical Metaphysics. Thesis, Stanford University, 1966.

Bauduer, J. B. Vie de Saint Grégoire de Nazianze, Archevêque de Constantinople. Paris, 1827.

Baur, L. "Untersuchungen über die Vergöttlichungslehre in der Theologie der griechischen Väter," Theologische Quartalschrift, 98 (1916), 99 (1918), 100 (1919), 101 (1920).

Benoit, A. Saint Grégoire de Nazianze: sa vie, ses oeuvres, son époque (2nd ed.). Paris, 1884.

Bernard, R. L'image de Dieu d'après Saint Athanase. Paris, 1952.

Bilaniuk, P. B. T. "The Mystery of Theosis and Divinization." Neiman, D. & Schatkin, M. (ed.),

The Heritage of the Early Church (Orientalia
Christiana Analecta, 195: Florovsky Festschrift.)
Rome, 1973.

Bornhaüser, K. Die Vergöttungslehre des Athanasius
und Johannes Damascenus. Gütersloh, 1903.

Bouyer, L. "Le problème du mal dans le Christianisme
antique." Dieu vivant, 6 (1946).

_____. La spiritualité du Nouveau Testament et des
Pères. Paris, 1960.

Butterworth, G. W. "The Deification of Man in Clement
of Alexandria." Journal of Theological Studies,
17 (1916).

Callahan, J. F. "Greek Philosophy and Cappadocian Cos-
mology." Dumbarton Oaks Papers, XII. Cambridge,
Mass., 1958.

Cameron, A. "Gregory of Nazianzus and Apollo." Journal
of Theological Studies (n.s.), 20.1 (1969).

Camelot, P. T. "Amour des lettres et désir de Dieu
chez Grégoire de Nazianze: Les Logoi au service
du Logos." Littérature et religion (Coppin Festschrift), Supplement to Mélanges de science religieuse, 22 (1966).

Capéran, L. Le problème du salut des infidèles: Essai
historique. Paris, 1912.

Cataudella, Q. "Gregorio Nazianzeno." Enciclopedia
Cattolica, 6. The Vatican, 1951.

Chadwick, H. Early Christian Thought and the Classical
Tradition. New York, 1966.

Chéné, J. "Unus de Trinitate passus est." Recherches
de science religieuse, 52 (1965).

Cherniss, H. F. The Platonism of Gregory of Nyssa.

(University of California Publications in Classical Philology, 11.) Berkeley, Calif., 1930.

Congar, Y. M.-J. "La déification dans la tradition spirituelle de l'Orient." Vie spirituelle. 43 (supplement: 1935).

Dalmais, I. & Bardy, G. "Divinisation." Dictionnaire de spiritualité ascétique et mystique, Vol. 3. Paris, 1957.

Danielou, J. The Angels and their Mission. Westminster, Md., 1957.

_____. "Les tuniques de peau chez Grégoire de Nysse." G. Muller & W. Zeller (ed.), Glaube, Geist, Geschichte (Benz Festschrift). Leiden, 1967.

_____. "Grégoire de Nysse à travers les lettres de Saint Basile et de Saint Grégoire de Nazianze." Vigiliae Christianae, 19 (1965).

_____. Platonisme et Théologie Mystique. Paris, 1953.

Des Places, E. Syngeneia: La parenté de l'homme avec Dieu d'Homère à la Patristique. Paris, 1964.

d'Herouville, P. "Quelque traces d'aristotélisme chez Grègoire de Nazianze." Recherches de science religieuse, 8 (1918).

Disdier, M. Th. "Bulletin bibliographique de la spiritualité byzantine et néo-grecque (1918-1931), Echos d'Orient, 32 (1931).

_____. "Nouvelles études sur saint Grégoire de Nazianze." Echos d'Orient, 30 (1931).

Dodds, E. R. Pagan and Christian in an Age of Anxiety. Cambridge, 1965.

Donders, A. Der Hl. Kirchenlehre Gregor von Nazianz als Homilet. Münster, 1909.

205

Dörries, H. De Spiritu Sancto. Göttingen, 1956.

Dräseke, J. "Gregorios von Nazianz und seine Verhältnis zum Apollinarismus." Theologische Studien und
Kritiken, 65 (1892).

Emmet, D. "Theoria and the Way of Life." Journal of
Theological Studies (n.s.), 17.1 (1966).

Ermoni, V. "La déification de l'homme chez les Pères
de l'Eglise." Revue du clergé francais, 9 (1897).

Faller, O. "Griechische Vergottung und christliche
Vergöttlichung." Gregorianum, 6 (1925).

Festugière, A. J. "Divinisation du chrétien." Vie
spirituelle, 59 (Supplément, 1939).

Fleury, E. Hellenisme et Christianisme: Saint Grégoire et son temps. Paris, 1930.

Florovsky, G. "Cur Deus Homo? The Motive of the Incarnation." Eucharisterion (Alivisatos Festschrift.)
Athens, 1958.

_____. Eastern Fathers of the Fourth Century (in
Russian). Paris, 1931.

_____. "The Lamb of God." The Scottish Journal of
Theology, 4 (1951).

_____. "The Resurrection of Life." Bulletin of the
Harvard University Divinity School, 49 (1952).

Franks, R. S. "The Idea of Salvation in the Theology
of the Eastern Church: A Study in the History of
Religion." Mansfield College Essays. London, 1909.

_____. The Work of Christ (2nd ed.). London, 1962.

Gallay, P. La vie de Saint Grégoire de Nazianze.
Paris, 1943.

Galtier, P. Le Saint Esprit en nous d'après les Pères grecs. (Analecta Gregoriana, Series Theologica, 35.A.4.) Rome, 1946.

Gillet, R. "L'homme divinisateur cosmique dans la pensée de saint Grégoire de Nysse." Studia Patristica (Texte und Untersuchungen, 81), 6.4.

Godet, P. "Grégoire de Nazianze." Dictionnaire de Théologie Catholique, 6. Paris, 1920.

Grenier, A. La vie et les poésies de Saint Grégoire de Nazianze. Clermont-Ferrand, 1858.

Grillmeier, A. Christ in Christian Tradition. London, 1964.

_____. "Quod non est assumptum—non sanatum." Lexicon für Theologie und Kirche, 8. Frieberg, 1963.

_____. "Die theologische und sprachliche Vorbereitung der christologischen Formel von Chalkedon." A. Grillmeier & H. Bacht (ed.), Das Konzil von Chalkedon. Würzburg, 1951.

Gross, J. La divinisation du chrétien d'après les Pères grecs. Paris, 1938.

_____. "Die Vergöttlichung des Christen nach den griechischen Vätern." Zeitschrift für Aszese und Mystik, 14 (1939).

Guignet, M. Saint Grégoire de Nazianze et la rhétorique. Paris, 1911.

Hanson, R. P. C. "Basil's Doctrine of Tradition in Relation to the Holy Spirit." Vigiliae Christianae, 22 (1968).

Harkianakis, S. "Die Trinitätslehre Gregors von Nazianz." Κληρονομία, 1 (1969).

Harnack, A. History of Dogma. New York, 1961.

Harnack, A. Die Terminologie der Wiedergeburt und verwandter Erlebnisse in der ältesten Kirche. (Texte und Untersuchungen, 43.3.) Leipzig, 1918.

Holl, K. Amphilochius von Ikonium in seinem Verhältnis zu den grossen Kappadoziern. Tubingen, 1904.

Karmiri, J. ἐκ τῆς ἐκκλησιολογίας τοῦ ἁγίου Γρεγορίου τοῦ Θεολόγου. Ekklesia, 36 (1959).

Korbacher, J. Ausserhalb der Kirche kein Heil? Munich, 1963.

Labriolle, P. La réaction païenne: Etude sur la polémique antichrétienne du Ier au VIe siècle. Paris, 1934.

Ladner, G. B. The Idea of Reform. Cambridge, Mass., 1959.

Lattey, C. "The Deification of Man in Clement of Alexandria: Some Further Notes." Journal of Theological Studies, 17 (1916).

Lietzmann, H. Apollinaris von Laodicea und seine Schule. Tübingen, 1904.

Lossky, V. The Mystical Theology of the Eastern Church. London, 1957.

_____. "Redemption and Deification." Sobornost, Ser. 3 (1947).

_____. The Vision of God. London, 1963.

Lot-Borodine, M. "La doctrine de la 'déification' dans l'Eglise Grecque jusqu'au XIe siècle." Revue de l'histoire des religions, 105 (1932), 106 (1932), 107 (1933).

Luneau, A. L'histoire de salut chez les Pères de l'Eglise. Paris, 1964.

Marechal, J. "Etudes sur la psychologie des mystiques," II. (Mus. Lessianum, Sect. Philos., 19.) Paris, 1937.

Martland, T. R. "A Study of Cappadocian and Augustinian Trinitarian Methodology." Anglican Theological Review, 47 (1965).

Martroye, F. "Le testament de Saint Grégoire de Nazianze." (Memoires de la Société Nationale des Antiquaires, Ser. 8, vol. 6.)

Meehan, D. "Editions of St. Gregory of Nazianzus." Irish Theological Quarterly, 18 (1951).

Merki, H. Ὁμοίωσις Θεοῦ - Von der Platonischen Angleichung an Gott zur Gottähnlichkeit bei Gregor von Nyssa. Freiburg, 1952.

Mersch, E. Le Corps Mystique du Christ (3rd ed.). Paris, 1951.

Michaud, E. "Ecclésiologie de St. Grégoire de Nazianze." Revue internationale de théologie, 12 (1904).

Misch, G. A History of Autobiography in Antiquity. Cambridge, Mass., 1951.

Momigliano, A. (ed.). The Conflict between Paganism and Christianity in the Fourth Century. Oxford, 1963.

Montaut, L. Revue critique de quelques questions historiques se rapportant à Saint Grégoire de Nazianze et son siècle. Paris, 1878.

Mossay, J. La mort et l'au-delà dans saint Grégoire de Nazianze. Louvain, 1966.

_____. "Perspectives eschatologiques de saint Grégoire de Nazianze." Questions liturgiques et paroissiales, 4 (1964).

Mühlenberg, E. Apollinaris von Laodicea. Göttingen, 1969.

Norris, R. A., Jr. Manhood and Christ. Oxford, 1963.

Otis, B. "Cappadocian Thought as a Coherent System." Dumbarton Oaks Papers, XII. Cambridge, Mass., 1958.

_____. "Nicene Orthodoxy and Fourth Century Mysticism." Actes du XIIe Congrès International d'Etudes Byzantines,2. Belgrade, 1964.

_____. "The Throne and the Mountain: An Essay on St. Gregory Nazianzus." Classical Journal, 56 (1961).

Patterson, L. G. "The Conversion of Diastēma in the Patristic View of Time." R. A. Norris, Jr. (ed.), Lux in Lumine: Essays to Honor W. Norman Pittenger. New York, 1966.

Philippou, A. J. "The Mystery of Pentecost." A. J. Philippou (ed.), The Orthodox Ethos ("Studies in Orthodoxy," 1). Oxford, 1964.

Pinault, H. Le Platonisme de Saint Grégoire de Nazianze: essai sur les relations du Christianisme et de l'Hellenisme dans son oeuvre théologique. La Roche-sur-Yon, 1925.

Plagnieux, J. "Saint Grégoire de Nazianze." Théologie de la vie monastique: études sur la tradition patristique. Paris, 1961.

_____. Saint Grégoire de Nazianze Théologien. Paris, 1951.

Prestige, G. L. God in Patristic Thought. London, 1951.

_____. Περιχωρέω and περιχώρησιſ in the Fathers," Journal of Theological Studies, 19 (1928).

Puech, A. Histoire de la littérature grecque chrétienne depuis les origines jusqu'à la fin du IVe siècle, 3. Paris, 1930.

Quéré, F. "Réflexions de Grégoire de Nazianze sur la parure féminine." Revue de science religieuse, 42 (1968).

Ritter, A. M. Das Konzil von Konstantinopel und sein Symbol. Studien zur Geschichte und Theologie des II Oekumenischen Konzils. Gottingen, 1965.

Rivière, J. Le dogme de la rédemption: essai d'étude historique. Paris, 1905.

_____. "Le marché avec le démon chez les Pères antérieurs à Saint Augustin." Revue de science religieuse, 8 (1928).

Rousse, J. "Les anges et leur ministère selon Saint Grégoire de Nazianze." Mélanges de science religieuse, 22 (1965).

_____. "Grégoire de Nazianze (saint)." Dictionnaire de Spiritualité, 6. Paris, 1967.

Ruether, R. R. Gregory of Nazianzus--Rhetor and Philosopher. Oxford, 1969.

Sabatier, A. La doctrine le l'expiation et son évolution historique. Paris, 1903.

Serra, M. "La carità pastorale in S. Gregorio Nazianzeno." Orientalia Christiana Periodica, 21 (1955).

Sinko, T. De traditione orationum Gregorii Nazianzeni. Cracow, 1917.

Slomkowski, A. L'état primitif de l'homme dans la tradition de l'église avant Saint Augustin. Paris, 1928.

Spidlik, T. Grégoire de Nazianze: Introduction à
l'étude de sa doctrine spirituelle. Rome, 1971.

Spindeler, A. Cur Verbum caro factum? Paderborn, 1938.

Stanescu, N. "Théologie et vie chez Saint Grégoire de
Nazianze." Mitropolia Olteniei,14 (1962).

Stephan, L. Die Soteriologie des Hl. Gregor von Nazianz. Vienna, 1938.

Szymusiak, J. "Amour de la solitude et vie dans la
monde à l'école de saint Grégoire de Nazianze."
La vie spirituelle, 114 (1966).

_____. Eléments de la théologie de l'homme selon
saint Grégoire de Nazianze. Rome, 1963.

_____. "Grégoire de Nazianze et le péché." Studia Pa-
tristica(Texte und Untersuchungen, 94), 9.

_____. Note sur l'amour des lettres au service de la
foi chrétienne chez Grégoire de Nazianze." Oikumene: Studi paleocristiani pubblicati in onore
del Concilio Ecumenico Vaticano II. University of
Catania, 1964.

_____. "Pour une chronologie des discours de S. Gré-
goire de Nazianze." Vigiliae Christianae, 20
(1966).

Telfer, W. "The Fourth Century Greek Fathers as Exe-
getes." Harvard Theological Review, 50 (1957).

Theodorou, A. "Die Lehre von der Vergottung des Menschen bei den griechischen Kirchenvätern." Kerygma
und Dogma, 7 (1961).

_____. Η περὶ θεώσεωſ τοῦ ανθρώπου διδασκάλια τῶν
ελλήνων πατέρων τῆſ εκκλησίαſ Ιωάννου τοῦ Δαμασ-
κηνοῦ. Athens, 1956.

Turmel, J. "Le dogme du péché originel avant Saint Augustin." Revue d'histoire et de littérature religieuses, 5 (1900).

_____. "L'eschatologie à la fin du IVe siècle." Revue d'histoire et de littérature religieuses, 5 (1900).

_____. "Histoire de l'angélologie dès temps apostoliques à la fin du Ve siècle." Revue d'histoire et de littérature religieuses, 2 (1898).

Turner, H. E. W. The Patristic Doctrine of Redemption. London, 1952.

_____. The Pattern of Truth. London, 1954.

Van Dale, R. L. An Understanding of Theosis in the Divine Liturgy and its Implications for the Ecumenical Church. Thesis, University of Iowa, 1968.

Volker, W. Gregor von Nyssa als Mystiker. Weisbaden, 1955.

Werner, M. Die Enstehung des christichen Dogmas (2nd ed.). Tübingen, 1941.

Wild, P. T. The Divinization of Man according to St. Hilary of Poitiers. Thesis, Saint Mary of the Lake Seminary, 1950.

Wiles, M. F. The Making of Christian Doctrine. Cambridge, 1967.

_____. "Psychological Analogies in the Fathers." Studia Patristica (Texte und Untersuchungen, 108), 11.

_____. "Soteriological Arguments in the Fathers." Studia Patristica (Texte und Untersuchungen, 94), 9.

_____. "The Unassumed in the Unhealed." Religious Studies, 4 (1968).

Williams, N. P. The Ideas of the Fall and of Original Sin. London, 1924.

Wilson, W. "The Genial Theologian: Gregory Nazianzen." The Popular Preachers of the Ancient Church. London (n.d.).

Winslow, D. F. "Christology and Exegesis in the Cappadocians." Church History, 40 (1971).

_____. "Gregory of Nazianzus and Love for the Poor." Anglican Theological Review, 47 (1965).

Wolfson, H. A. "Philosophical Implications of Arianism and Apollinarianism." Dumbarton Oaks Papers, XII. Cambridge, Mass., 1958.

_____. The Philosophy of the Church Fathers, 1 (2nd ed.). Cambridge, Mass., 1964.

Young, F. M. "Christological Ideas in the Greek Commentaries on the Epistle to the Hebrews." Journal of Theological Studies (n.s.), 20.1 (1969).

_____. "A Reconsideration of Alexandrian Christology." Journal of Ecclesiastical History, 22.2 (1971).